T0328783

Cambridge Elements ☰

Elements in Philosophy and Logic
edited by
Bradley Armour-Garb
SUNY Albany
Frederick Kroon
The University of Auckland

THE MANY FACES OF IMPOSSIBILITY

Koji Tanaka
Australian National University

Alexander Sandgren
Independent Scholar

CAMBRIDGE
UNIVERSITY PRESS

CAMBRIDGE
UNIVERSITY PRESS

Shaftesbury Road, Cambridge CB2 8EA, United Kingdom

One Liberty Plaza, 20th Floor, New York, NY 10006, USA

477 Williamstown Road, Port Melbourne, VIC 3207, Australia

314–321, 3rd Floor, Plot 3, Splendor Forum, Jasola District Centre,
New Delhi – 110025, India

103 Penang Road, #05–06/07, Visioncrest Commercial, Singapore 238467

Cambridge University Press is part of Cambridge University Press & Assessment,
a department of the University of Cambridge.

We share the University's mission to contribute to society through the pursuit of
education, learning and research at the highest international levels of excellence.

www.cambridge.org
Information on this title: www.cambridge.org/9781009485944

DOI: 10.1017/9781009180573

First published 2024

A catalogue record for this publication is available from the British Library.

ISBN 978-1-009-48594-4 Hardback
ISBN 978-1-009-18058-0 Paperback
ISSN 2516-418X (online)
ISSN 2516-4171 (print)

The Many Faces of Impossibility

Elements in Philosophy and Logic

DOI: 10.1017/9781009180573
First published online: February 2024

Koji Tanaka
Australian National University

Alexander Sandgren
Independent Scholar

Author for correspondence: Koji Tanaka, Koji.Tanaka@anu.edu.au

Abstract: *Possible worlds* have revolutionised philosophy and some related fields. But, in recent years, tools based on possible worlds have been found to be limited in many respects. *Impossible worlds* have been introduced to overcome these limitations. This Element aims to raise and answer the neglected question of what is characteristically impossible about impossible worlds. The Element sheds new light on the nature of impossible worlds. It also aims to analyse the main features and utility of impossible worlds and examine how impossible worlds can capture distinctions which are unavailable if we limit ourselves to possible world-based tools.

Keywords: impossible worlds, logical impossibility, non-normal worlds, non-classical logic, hyperintentionality, counterpossibles

ISBNs: 9781009485944 (HB), 9781009180580 (PB), 9781009180573 (OC)
ISSNs: 2516-418X (online), 2516-4171 (print)

Contents

1 Introduction

It is not too much of an exaggeration to say that *possible worlds* revolutionised philosophy and some related fields. They have afforded tools that are used to analyse *intensional* concepts such as modality (possibility and necessity), meaning, information, belief and knowledge to name a few. By capturing ways things might be, or might be said to be, known to be or believed to be, possible worlds have allowed fine-grained distinctions that could not be adequately captured with merely extensional resources, that is, resources based on what things there actually are. Possible worlds are now indispensable theoretical tools in logic and metaphysics but they are also used in many other areas of philosophy including the philosophy of language, the philosophy of mind, epistemology, the philosophy of computation, metaethics, the philosophy of science as well as related areas such as artificial intelligence, linguistics, mathematics, and physics.

These useful and valuable tools have, however, been found to be limited in many respects. Possible worlds are not sufficient to allow for even finer-grained distinctions. This is because, in many contexts, distinctions must be made between necessarily equivalent contents. For instance, consider the following:

(i) If you apply for the job, you have a 80 per cent chance of not getting it.

(ii) If you apply for the job, you have a 20 per cent chance of getting it.

Given that (i) and (ii) convey the same information, they are necessarily equivalent. But some may be more likely to believe that they should apply for the job after hearing (ii) than after hearing (i) because of the framing effect (Tversky & Kahneman (1981)). This suggests that we (humans) believe different things about necessarily equivalent matters.

Phenomena such as this have come to be known as *hyperintensional* phenomena. Hyperintensional phenomena occur in situations in which necessarily equivalents cannot be substituted while preserving truth. A common idea is that if we are going to account for hyperintensional phenomena, the standard possible worlds apparatus needs to be extended. One strategy to accommodate hyperintensionality is to introduce *impossible worlds* across which necessarily equivalent contents may not be equivalent (Berto & Jago (2019), Berto & Nolan (2021), Jago (2014), Nolan (2014)). This strategy is certainly not the only option. One might treat hyperintensional phenomena to be somehow linguistic and give an expressivist treatment in terms of *counterconventions* (Kocurek & Jerzak (2021)). Or one might analyse hyperintentional phenomena in terms of *metalinguistic negotiations* (Kouri Kissel (2019)). And, one can always deny that hyperintensional phenomena are genuine (T. Williamson (2007, 2013, 2020, 2021)). Nevertheless, the importance of impossible worlds has slowly been recognised.

One does not have to be committed to the reality of hyperintentional phenomena to see the value of impossible worlds. If one recognises that impossibility is a modal notion, gaining an understanding of modality should involve an understanding not only of possibility but also of impossibility. Hence, the study of impossibility is valuable not only in the context of accounting for hyperintentionality but in the context of understanding modality.

While the importance of impossible worlds has gradually become more widely recognised,[1] the question of what is characteristically impossible about impossible worlds has not received much attention. An impossible world is a world that 'contains' or represents impossibility. But, beyond this general description, there does not seem to be an agreement about what makes a world impossible. From a perspective of classical logic, a world where a contradiction obtains may be an impossible world. However, from a perspective of paraconsistent logic where contradictions are accommodated in a sensible manner, some such contradictory worlds may not be impossible. So, in order to come to a neutral understanding of impossible worlds, we need a definition that is logic-neutral in the sense that the definition does not rely on any particular logic.[2]

In raising a question about impossible worlds, we will focus on *logically* impossible worlds. In particular, we will analyse logical impossibility by being neutral about which logic is correct (holds at the actual world). In so doing, we will also remain neutral about the ontological and metaphysical nature of impossible worlds. Thus, we are not concerned with the existence or non-existence of impossible worlds or the genuine or ersatz nature of impossible worlds.[3] Rather, the question we are mainly interested in is: given a world, if it is impossible, what makes it so? Hence, the focus will not be on impossible *worlds* but on the *impossibility* of impossible worlds.

In literature on impossible worlds, we can find three features that have been taken to be characteristic of what makes a world impossible[4]:

---

[1] See, for instance, Berto & Jago (2019, 2022) as well as Sections 7–8 of this Element.

[2] For the definitions of impossible worlds that rely on classical logic or classical consistency, see Bjerring (2013, 2014), Goodman (2004), Nolan (1997), and Zalta (1997).

[3] For some of the metaphysical issues concerning impossible worlds, see Berto & Jago (2019: chs. 2 and 3), Kiourti (2019), Vander Laan (1997), and Yagisawa (2010).

[4] For different classifications of definitions of impossible worlds, see Berto & Jago (2019, 2022), Jago (2013b), and Nolan (2013).

1. *Difference*: a difference in the laws of logic (Priest (1992, 2008, 202+))
2. *Openness*: failure of closure under any set of logical laws (Berto & Jago (2019), Priest (2005, 202+))
3. *Violation*: the presence of a violation of some set of logical laws (Sandgren & Tanaka (2020), Tanaka (2018), Tanaka & Girard (2023))

As we will see, these features have not been clearly distinguished and they are often treated as equivalent and used interchangeably. However, they can and should be distinguished. Once we make these distinctions, we can come to appreciate that there are different kinds of impossible worlds that have been introduced and that they do different things.

In this Element, we aim to do two things. In Sections 3–6, we will introduce and distinguish the key features that have been purported to be characteristic of impossible worlds. The first part of the Element will, thus, shed new light on impossible worlds by clarifying what, exactly, is impossible about them. In Sections 7–8, we will analyse the various theoretical roles impossible worlds have been introduced to play and discuss what features impossible worlds must have to play those roles. As such, the second part of the Element will include a survey of the literature on impossible worlds. But it won't be a survey from a neutral perspective. Rather, it will be an opinionated examination of the main features and utility of impossible worlds based on the distinctions between difference, openness, and violation that are introduced and analysed in Sections 3–6. Given that an understanding of the impossibility of impossible worlds requires those distinctions (as will be shown in Sections 3–6) and that such distinctions have not been recognised in the literature, there cannot be a non-opinionated examination of impossible worlds. Even though it is opinionated, the survey will provide insight into whether and how impossible worlds can capture various phenomena such as hyperintensionality and, more generally, what they can and cannot do in the context of discussions of modality and various modal notions.

2 Conceptual Prolegomenon

Some important concepts need to be laid out at the outset. Some of these concepts have not been made explicit in the literature on impossible worlds (at least not to our satisfaction). Before considering the issue of what makes impossible worlds impossible, we will lay out some of them here as we will refer to them throughout the Element.

2.1 Modality: Absolute vs. Relative

It is customary and, in fact, the contemporary orthodoxy to represent modality, in particular, necessity and possibility, in terms of *possible worlds*. Modal claims (necessity and possibility claims) are assessed not only by what is actually the case but by reference to the 'space' of possible worlds. We assume that there is a set of possible worlds each representing a way things could be. We then evaluate modal claims as follows.

- A necessity claim, $\Box A$ (A is necessarily the case), is true iff A is true at *all* relevant possible worlds.
- A possibility claim, $\Diamond A$ (A is possibly the case), is true iff A is true at *some* relevant possible world.

Depending on what counts as relevant, we may place a constraint on the 'space' of possible worlds. By varying the constraint, we would generate different (normal) modal logics such as C. I. Lewis' *S4* and *S5* (C. I. Lewis (1918)) – at least, we would generate the semantics that are sound and complete with respect to C. I. Lewis' (normal) modal logics. What is important here is that an assessment of the truth values of modal claims depends not only on what the worlds are like but also how they relate to each other. Hence, the notions of necessity and possibility used in the semantics for evaluating modal claims is a *relative* notion. A world may be necessary or possible *relative to* a given world.

However, it is also part of the contemporary orthodoxy that a set of possible worlds used in evaluating modal claims is not an unstructured body of 'dots' or 'points'. It is more like a structured web. The necessity or possibility of a claim is taken to depend on the structure of the set of worlds which is, in turn, taken to have a necessary structure. Importantly, this structure is often assumed to be *pluriversal* in that the set of worlds as a whole has a necessary structure. This is one of the reasons why many take the structure of the space of possible worlds to support the inferences associated with *S4* (or stronger) like $\Box p \models \Box\Box p$ and $\Diamond\Diamond p \models \Diamond p$ (or the axioms associated with *S4* like $\Box p \to \Box\Box p$ and $\Diamond\Diamond p \to \Diamond p$).

When impossible worlds are included, one may still hold that what counts as impossible is part of the necessary structure of the whole modal space.[5] This means that if something is impossible given the whole space of worlds, it is impossible in some *absolute* sense. Roughly speaking, the absolutists will contend that the line between the impossible and the possible does not depend on which world we are evaluating a modal claim from; rather, the line is drawn by the overall structure of the modal space.

This absolute sense of possibility and impossibility holds even in the context of counterfactuals. A counterfactual is a conditional whose antecedent concerns what may not actually be but could be.[6] The standard semantics to account for

---

[5] For instance, Nolan (1997) and Priest (2016a).

[6] How to define a counterfactual is a controversial issue and we do not have a stake in that issue. We present a counterfactual in this way as a working definition.

counterfactuals (Kratzer (1977), D. Lewis (1973), Stalnaker (1968)) evaluates them in terms of the *most similar* or *closest* worlds where the antecedent is true. This means that it requires the worlds or the points of evaluations to be ordered in terms of similarity or closeness relation between worlds. As has been claimed by D. Lewis and others, this relation is context sensitive. That is, there is no one fixed or absolute way to order the worlds. Nevertheless, it might be thought that, once the worlds are ordered in a context, the division between possible and impossible worlds might be drawn by the overall structure given by the ordering. Hence, a world may be impossible in an *absolute* sense even if the overall structure is context sensitive.

2.2 Non-normal Worlds

When C. I. Lewis introduced modal logics, he introduced not only *S4* and *S5*, so called *normal* modal logics, but also *non-normal* modal logics such as *S2* and *S3*.[7] These systems are weaker than more familiar normal modal systems and, as a result, modality is treated in a way that may be unfamiliar to contemporary audience.

The primary characteristic of the non-normal systems is the failure of necessitation: it is not always the case that if $\models A$ then $\models \Box A$. In a normal system, a necessity claim, $\Box A$, is evaluated in terms of the truth value of A at *all* relevant worlds. So, if A is true at all worlds (and, thus, $\models A$), then A is true at all relevant worlds. So $\Box A$ is true at all worlds. Thus, $\models \Box A$. Hence, in a normal system, if $\models A$ then $\models \Box A$.

In order to capture the failure of necessitation semantically, Kripke (1965) introduced *non-normal worlds* where $\Box A$ fails to hold for any A. (By the interchangeability of $\Box\neg$ and $\neg\Diamond$ which holds in non-normal systems, $\Diamond A$ is true for every A at a non-normal world.) Validity, $\models$, is defined in terms of truth preservation at all *normal* worlds.[8] Since $B \vee \neg B$ is true at every world for any B, $\models B \vee \neg B$. At a non-normal world, however, $\Box(B \vee \neg B)$ fails to hold. Hence, it is not the case that $\models \Box(B \vee \neg B)$. Non-normal worlds, thus, capture the failure of necessitation.

The idea of non-normal worlds was generalised by Routley & Meyer (1973) in the semantics for relevant logics (which is an extension of the semantics for *First Degree Entailment* (FDE) introduced by Routley & Routley

---

[7] He also introduced *S1*. However, an appropriate semantics was found to be difficult to find and it needs to be treated slightly differently from other non-normal modal logics. See Cresswell (1995) for a semanmtics for *S1*.

[8] This is the case in C. I. Lewis' systems. The systems of Lemmon (1957), *E2* and *E3*, define validity in terms of *all* worlds.

(1972)). In relevant logics, $A \rightarrow (B \rightarrow B)$ should come out invalid because A and $B \rightarrow B$ are irrelevant (they do not share any propositional variables). This means that there must be a way for $B \rightarrow B$ to fail to be true while A is true in the semantics. However, $B \rightarrow B$ is a logical truth in (most) relevant logics. So, there must be a way for a logical truth to fail in order to invalidate $A \rightarrow (B \rightarrow B)$. Routley & Meyer used non-normal worlds to achieve this effect.

The way that Routley & Meyer invalidated $A \rightarrow (B \rightarrow B)$ is as follows. At a non-normal world, the truth value of a conditional, $A \rightarrow B$, is not determined by the truth values of A and B at the same world. It is determined by those values at worlds that are different but related in a ternary manner. What is important here is not the ternary relations as such but the fact that the antecedent and the consequent of a conditional are evaluated at different worlds. That allows $B \rightarrow B$ to fail to be true at a non-normal world. So, the introduction of non-normal worlds was vital for the development of relevant logics.[9]

2.3 Entailment Statements

In order to talk about the logical characteristics of a world that contains logical impossibility, we assume that there are logical laws that hold *at* a world and that we have a language to express them. These assumptions need to be shown to be cogent (Priest (202+)). In this Element, however, we take these assumptions to be in place.

When logical laws hold at a world, we say that there is a set of *entailment schemas* that represent the laws. An entailment schema takes the form: $A_1, A_2, \ldots \models B_1, B_2, \ldots$ where A_i and B_i are meta-variables meaning that they are atomic propositions or complex formulas.[10] If $A_1, A_2, \ldots \models B_1, B_2, \ldots$ holds at w, then B_i takes a 'good' value for some i at w when A_i takes a 'good' value for all i at w. Alternatively, if A_i takes a 'good' value for all i at w, then B_i does *not* take a 'bad' value for any i at w. What count as 'good' and 'bad' values depends on the logic in question. But, in general, a 'good' value is the one that is preserved in a valid inference and a 'bad' value is one that forms part of a counterexample to a valid inference. For illustrative purposes, we say that if A takes a good value, it is *true*, and if A takes a bad value, it is *non-true*. We simply take truth and non-truth to represent good and bad values understood

---

[9] For this way of describing the achievement of Routley & Meyer, see Priest (1992) and Tanaka (2013, 2018).

[10] To generalise this to cover (full) relevant logics (whose languages allow nested relevant conditionals), one can think of a law to be expressed by some relevant conditional. See Priest (202+).

in terms of validity and counterexample respectively. What exactly truth and non-truth amount to is a contentious question but we need not settle it here.[11]

Then, an *entailment statement* is an instance of an entailment schema.[12] It specifies a valid inference according to a logical law. For instance, if $A \wedge B \models A$ is a logical law, its instance such as $p \wedge q \models p$ is an entailment statement. For simplicity, we assume that the language for the statements is propositional. We also assume that the language for the entailment statements does not contain a conditional. This is to avoid the issue that comes up in the context of relevant logics, especially in the context of nested relevant conditionals.

Counterexamples to an entailment schema $A_1, A_2, \ldots \models B_1, B_2, \ldots$ at a world w are $p_1, p_2, \ldots$ and $q_1, q_2, \ldots$ that hold at w such that p_i and q_i are propositions (or whatever the truth bearers are) and that p_i and q_i can be used to instantiate $A_1, A_2, \ldots \models B_1, B_2, \ldots$ where all the premises are true and the conclusions non-true. For instance, let's assume that Identity ($A \models A$) holds at w. Suppose that p is both true and non-true. Then, an instance of $A \models A$, $p \models p$, takes you from truth to non-truth. So, if $A \models A$ holds at w, p is a counterexample to Identity at w.[13]

2.4 Logical Humean Supervenience

We assume that a world w consists of a set of entailment statements that specify valid inferences and a set of (non-logical) facts that hold at w. For the purposes of this Element, we do not need to go into answering what facts are. We just take them to be represented by propositions. So, if $A_1, A_2, \ldots \models B_1, B_2, \ldots$ is a logical law that holds at a world, we let, for instance, $p_1, p_2, \ldots \models q_1, q_2, \ldots$ represent a valid inference and $p_i, q_i, \ldots$ represent facts that hold at the world. If an entailment schema $A_1, A_2, \ldots \models B_1, B_2, \ldots$ has counterexamples at a world w, there are instances of it such that those instances have premises which are true at w and conclusions that are non-true at w. However, if the entailment schema holds at w, then $B_1, B_2, \ldots$ must be true for some B_i when A_is are all true. So, the presence of counterexamples implies that some *instances* of the laws of logic (expressed by entailment statements) do not obey the laws.

If a world contains a counterexample, what we call Logical Humean Supervenience (LHS), fails at that world:

> *Logical Humean Supervenience:* The laws of logic that hold at a world supervene on their instances at that world.

---

[11] For some discussions on this question, see Tanaka & Girard (2023) and Weber (2021).

[12] Thanks go to an anonymous referee for pointing out that we have to separate entailment *statements* from entailment *schemas*.

[13] See Sandgren & Tanaka (2020) and Tanaka & Girard (2023).

We are conceiving of a world to consist of a set of entailment statements and a set of (non-logical) facts. An entailment statement is an instance of a law of logic. We can think of it as representing the logical 'qualities' of the (non-logical) facts that hold at the world. From a logical point of view, a world consists of those 'qualities'. So a world is 'a vast mosaic of local matters of particular fact' and nothing more, to use the phrase of D. Lewis (1986: ix). When a law of logic holds at a world, it supervenes on the 'arrangement of [logical] qualities' (D. Lewis (1986: ix)).

Now, LHS ensures that all the worlds are logically 'well-behaved'. If LHS is in place, there is no world such that, for instance, p and q are true but $p \land q$ is non-true while Conjunction Introduction $(A, B \models A \land B)$ holds at that world. So, there would not be any world where it is raining and the grass is wet but it is non-true that it is raining *and* the grass is wet. LHS rules out such a world. Hence, the presence of counterexamples often signals a schism between the logical laws and what happens at a world. We will see in Sections 3–6 that LHS plays a crucial role in separating different accounts of impossible worlds (or the impossibility of impossible worlds).

2.5 Non-classical Logics

Classical logic is a logic that was devised by Frege, Russell, and Hilbert at the turn of the twentieth century. A *non-classical logic* is a logic that does not validate some of the laws of classical logic. This means that a set of non-classical laws may not correspond to the set of classical laws. We will be using one kind of non-classical logics as an example in this Element. That is *paraconsistent logic*. This is because a contrast can be seen rather sharply when we compare classical logic and paraconsistent logic.[14] Classical logic is a logic that validates *ex contradictione quodlibet* (ECQ): $A, \neg A \models B$ for any A and B. Classically, everything (that can be expressed by the given language) is a valid consequence of a contradiction. This means that, classically, if a contradiction holds at a world, such a world is a trivial world, that is, a world where everything (expressible in the language) holds. A *paraconsistent logic* is a logic that does not validate ECQ. This means that, paraconsistently, even if a world contains a contradiction, it may not be a trivial world. If a world is trivial, that is not because everything is a consequence of a contradiction. Hence, a paraconsistent logic is a logic that can circumvent a contradiction from spreading everywhere (hence, non-explosive).[15]

---

[14] It is also the case that impossible worlds are often discussed in the presence of paraconsistent logic.

[15] For an introduction to paraconsistent logic, see, for instance, Priest, Tanaka, & Weber (2022).

3 Difference

Priest (1992) used the terminology 'impossible words' to describe non-normal worlds. As we saw in §2.2, the non-normal worlds were used to capture the formal semantics for C. I. Lewis' non-normal modal systems such as *S2* and *S3* (Kripke (1965)) as well as the worlds introduced by Routley et al. (1982) for the semantics for relevant logics. In describing these worlds as impossible, Priest characterised the impossibility of worlds in terms of logical *difference*. Under this characterisation, if the laws of logic that hold at the actual world are classical, a world where a non-classical logic holds is, for this reason, an impossible world. The idea that logical difference is central to understanding impossibility has been influential.[16]

What is a logical difference? A world w_1 is logically *different* from w_2 if the set of entailment schemas that hold at w_1 is different from those that hold at w_2. Suppose that the entailment schemas that hold at w_1 correspond exactly to those that are classically valid and those that hold at w_2 correspond exactly to those that are valid according to some paraconsistent logic. That is, $A, \neg A \models B$ (ECQ) holds at w_1 but does not hold at w_2. This means that w_2 would not be a trivial world (a world where everything holds) even if a contradiction were to obtain (unless w_2 was trivial from the start) whereas w_1 would be a trivial world if it contains a contradiction and is closed. In this case, w_1 and w_2 are logically different worlds.

How is difference supposed to be characteristic of impossibility? Priest develops the idea that difference is the key to account for impossibility via an analogy to the laws of physics (or the laws of nature). In this section, we will follow this development. We will then examine what is involved in this analogy and critically assess whether or not the analogy establishes logical difference as characteristic of impossible worlds.

3.1 An Analogy to Physics

Priest (1992) motivates the characterisation of impossibility in terms of difference by an analogy to the laws of physics (or nature).

> There are ... worlds where there are differences of a much more profound sort where, for example, the laws of nature are different; where, e.g., things can travel faster than the speed of light. ... But just as there are possible worlds where the laws of physics are different, so there are possible worlds where the laws of logic are different. (p. 292)

---

[16] See Mares (1997), Priest (2008, 202+), and Restall (1997).

Priest then calls such worlds 'logically impossible worlds':

> By analogy with the case where the laws of physics are different, we might
> call worlds where the laws of logic are different logically impossible worlds.
> (p. 292)

Having suggested that impossible worlds are logically different worlds and appealing to this analogy to the laws of physics, Priest does not step through the analogy to show what lessons can be drawn from it. In order to judge the adequacy of the analogy and, in turn, the characterisation of impossible worlds as logically different worlds, we must unpack the analogy.

The analogy seems to go as follows. It is a law of physics (or nature) at the actual world that no one can travel faster than the speed of light. So it may be a physical possibility that Usain Bolt keeps breaking world records but a physical impossibility that he accelerates past the speed of light (at least, this is what the analogy assumes). However, at a physically impossible world, the laws of physics at that world may allow Usain Bolt to accelerate indefinitely and run faster than the speed of light. The physically impossible Olympics would be a spectacular event (though mostly unobservable). This is the case even if he does not break any records at that world, or run faster than the speed of light at that world, etc.[17] The thought is that the laws of physics at that impossible world allow Usain Bolt to accelerate past the speed of light even if he may not do so at that world but that the laws of physics at the actual world do not make this allowance. That impossible world and our world must, thus, be governed by different physical laws.

Analogously, a logically impossible world is a world where the laws of logic are different, in particular, from the actual world. If classical logic holds at the actual world, then a world where a paraconsistent logic holds is a logically different world. Thus, if classical logic holds at the actual world, a world where paraconsistent logic holds is an impossible world.

But what makes these logically (and physically) different worlds impossible? In the case of physical impossibility, the laws of physics (or nature) at the actual world dictate that no one can travel faster than the speed of light. Relative to the actual laws of physics, then, it is a physical impossibility that Usain Bolt arrives at the end of the track before light gets there. Similarly, if the actual world is a classical world, relative to the actual laws of logic, it is a logical impossibility that ECQ is invalid.

---

[17] See Priest (1992: §5, 2008: §9.7).

To make this point clear, consider the following analogy which reflects Priest's more recent thought about the issue.[18] Let's suppose that 'all lumps of gold are less than 100 kg' is contingently true at the actual world. Now imagine a world that is exactly the same as the actual world, except that there is a law of physics (or nature) to the effect that all lumps of gold more than or equal to 100 kg explode. Since there is a law that holds in that world but does not hold in the actual world, it is a physically different world. In such a physically different world, there being a 101 kg stable lump of gold is impossible. However, it is possible that there is a stable 101 kg lump of gold at the actual world even though there is, as a matter of contingent fact, no such lump. In such a case, the only difference between the two worlds is the difference of the laws of physics (or nature). So, what explains the possibility and impossibility of a stable 101 kg lump of gold is the difference of the laws of physics (or nature) at the two worlds. Similarly, so the analogy goes, ECQ being invalid is impossible at a classical world but it is possible at a paraconsistent world, even if there are no true contradictions at either world. Given that those two worlds may be the same except the difference in their laws, it is difference that is the mark of impossibility, or so it is argued.

3.2 Is Difference the Mark of Impossibility?

There are three things that should be noted about this characterisation of impossibility and the analogy to the laws of physics (or nature). First, the analogy makes use of the relative notion of possibility and impossibility. Whether Usain Bolt accelerating past the speed of light is possible or impossible is described as relative to a world: it is possible relative to a world where there is no law to the effect that he cannot run faster than the speed of light but impossible relative to the actual world and its laws. Indeed, the absolute sense of difference, difference-full-stop, does not make sense; difference is always difference *from* something. Thus, if we characterise impossible worlds in terms of difference, impossibility is given a *modal* characterisation: describing a world as impossible requires a reference to other worlds, or other points of evaluation, in modal space.[19]

Second, physically or logically different worlds are individuated by different sets of laws. On this story, what makes a world impossible is not what happens at the world but the impossibility of the laws of physics (or nature) in

---

[18] The analogy given here is the one that was presented to us by Graham Priest in personal communication. By his own admission, it reflects his current thought better than what he had said before.

[19] Many thanks go to an anonymous reviewer for pointing this out.

comparison to a different set of laws. Similarly, what makes a paraconsistent world impossible (assuming that the actual world is classical) is the laws of logic that hold at the world irrespective of the behaviour of the instances of the laws at that world. So, the analogy characterises the impossibility of impossible worlds in terms of some set of laws themselves being impossible.

Third (which is a consequence of the second), the notion of difference applies to the laws and it is the laws that determine what the worlds are like. In the case of physically different worlds, the difference between the actual world and the physically different world appealed to in the analogy concerns a law that no one can travel faster than the speed of light. Moreover, at the actual world where there is a law to the effect that no one can travel faster than the speed of light, no one indeed travels faster than the speed of light. But Usain Bolt may beat the speed of light in a physically different world where there is no such law. So, the analogy suggests that laws supervene on what happens at the world. For instance, if Usain Bolt were to run faster than the speed of light, it would have to be in the physically impossible world rather than in the actual world that he would do so. Analogously, the measure of difference in the context of logic is the difference of the laws of logic. The analogy compares a classical world and a paraconsistent world without any consideration of what instances of the laws might obtain at those worlds. So, the analogy presupposes LHS; that is, that there is no mismatch between the laws and their instances that obtain at any of the worlds.

3.3 What Difference Does Difference Make?

The three points discussed in the previous section seem to come in conflict with other desiderata identified in the literature. In this section, we will discuss two such desiderata. We will not resolve them or use them to argue against difference as the mark of impossibility here; however, they should be kept in mind when we consider applications of impossible worlds in Sections 7–8.

(1) Despite the fact that the analogy makes use of the relative sense of impossibility, the notion of difference in play presupposes the absolute sense of impossibility. Consider all of the physically different worlds which are characterised in terms of the difference of the laws of physics (or nature) from those of the actual world. If we metaphorically think of these worlds as scattered around the space of all physically different worlds, the space represents all the ways in which the laws of physics (or nature) might or might not be centred around the actual world. Among them are impossible worlds such as the one where there is no law to the effect that no one can run faster than the speed of light. This means that, given the universe of all the physically possible worlds

centred around the actual world, some regions of the universe are conceived to contain impossible worlds. Thus, the notion of impossibility in play is absolute: a world is impossible if it resides in the region of the whole modal space which is identified as impossible.

Without this absolute sense of impossibility, it is hard to see how there is any impossibility involved in the analogy. To see this, consider the second analogy about the lumps of gold. After the actual world is described as a world where 'all lumps of gold are less than 100 kg' is contingently true, a physically different world is introduced as representing a way in which things *could* be. As Priest says, 'there are possible worlds where the laws of logic are different' (Priest (1992: 292)). So it is introduced as a *possible* world relative to the actual world. The only way to count this physically different world as impossible is to introduce the absolute sense of impossibility and claim that it is impossible because it occupies a certain region of the modal space where impossible worlds reside.

(2) Nolan (1997) holds the following principle in advocating impossible worlds:

> If A is impossible, there is at least one impossible world where A holds.[20]

If A is possible, there is at least one possible world where A holds. So, Nolan's principle is equivalent to

> For any A, there is at least one world where A holds.

Nolan (1997) thinks of this principle as unrestricted comprehension.

Priest (2016a) adopts a stronger principle:

> For any A, there is at least one world where A holds and there is at least one world where A fails.[21]

Priest's principle is stronger as it says not only about the worlds where A holds but also the worlds where A fails.[22] Priest calls this principle the 'Primary Directive' and presents it as the 'leading principle of impossible-world semantics' (Priest (2016a: 2653)).[23]

---

[20] In his own words, 'for every proposition which cannot be true, there is an impossible world where that proposition is true' (Nolan (1997: 542)).

[21] In his own words: 'Everything holds at some worlds, and everything fails at some worlds' (Priest (2016a: 2653)).

[22] See Berto & Jago (2019: 174)).

[23] Priest's Second Directive is even stronger: 'If A and B are distinct formulas, there are worlds where A holds and B fails' (Priest (2016a: 2655)). In this Element, we are concerned only with

We call Priest's principle the *unrestricted comprehension principle* (because that sounds more like a principle). Given unrestricted comprehension, there will be at least one world where A holds but there is at least one world where A fails even though the laws of logic that hold at those worlds are the same. So, at some worlds, there will be a discrepancy between the laws and what happens at a world (including the instances of a given set of laws). Hence, according to the unrestricted comprehension principle, LHS must fail in that the laws do not supervene on their instances.

In order to rule out a world where there is such a mismatch between the laws and their instances, one might reject unrestricted comprehension principle. In fact, Priest (202+) suggests exactly this:

> We have an actual world, @, and a bunch of other worlds. [L] is a language adequate for describing what holds at worlds, *with – perhaps – the exception of the facts about logical consequence.*[24]

The exclusion of the facts about the laws of logic from constituting worlds is a way of constraining the laws that hold at worlds. This allows logical qualities of (non-logical) facts to always match or obey the laws in that it allows us to exclude the worlds where the laws and their instances come apart. This modification would restore LHS.

However, removing the worlds at which instances do not match the laws from the picture raises a tension in the dialectic. One motivation for introducing impossible worlds is to account for hyperintensional phenomena where necessary equivalents can be distinguished. Restricting the worlds so that the laws and their instances match at *all* worlds imposes a kind of necessary structure over the whole modal space which the introduction of impossible worlds is meant to counteract in the context of hyperintentionality. So, excluding the worlds where the laws and their instances come apart undermines the very motivation for introducing impossible worlds. Hence, if we are to account for hyperintensionality generally, we should not rule out worlds at which the laws and their instances come apart and, thus, we should reject LHS.[25]

Thus, characterising impossible worlds as logically different worlds conflicts with some of the desiderata that the introduction of impossible worlds is meant to accommodate. Whether or not this means that impossible worlds should not be characterised as logically different worlds is a question we leave

---

the Primary Directive. For a discussion of the Second Directive, see Berto & Jago (2019: §8.4) and Tanaka (202+).

[24] Our emphasis.

[25] See also Kiourti (2019).

to the side for now. However, the above discussion shows that such a characterisation cannot be motivated solely by the 'intuitive' appeal of an analogy to physics (or nature).

4 Openness

Open worlds were introduced to address issues that arise in the context of *intentionality* (Priest (2005)). Intentionality is a feature of mental states (and other representations) that are directed at or about things. It is a feature of many mental states including knowledge, beliefs, fear, hopes, love, and hatred.[26] These mental states are often not closed under logical consequence. For instance, suppose that $p \vee \neg p$ is a tautology and that q is a complex truth that logically follows from $p \vee \neg p$ but that no one has ever considered. Then one might believe $p \vee \neg p$ without believing q (Priest (2005: 20)). In such a case, our beliefs are not closed under logical consequence. For another example, consider knowledge. Let K be a knowledge operator. If we analyse K as a modal operator just like the necessity operator $\Box$ (see Hintikka (1962)), then the following closure principle holds:

If KA and $A \models B$, then KB.

It says that if an agent knows that A, then they must also know all of the logical consequences of A. In other words, the agent who satisfies this principle is logically omniscient. There is, thus, the problem of logical omniscience as no human is logically omniscient. One way to model knowledge of human agents is to use open worlds so that the above closure principle fails.[27] Open worlds were introduced to model such intentional operators.[28]

Now, Priest (2005) introduced open worlds in addition to 'impossible worlds'. An 'impossible world' in Priest (2005) is a world that accounts for the failure of $B \rightarrow B$ in certain contexts in relevant logics which is required to invalidate the irrelevant conditional $A \rightarrow (B \rightarrow B)$. However, such a world is closed under some logic since it is closed under *modus ponens*.[29] So, open worlds are not what he once called 'impossible worlds'.

Since then, however, open worlds have become paradigmatic worlds to motivate the idea of impossible worlds for some. Berto, French, Priest, &

---

[26] See, for instance, Jacob (2023).

[27] See Berto & Jago (2019: ch. 5), Priest (2005: ch. 1), and Rantala (1982a, 1982b). Bjerring (2013) introduces worlds that are different in kind from open worlds to invalidate the closure principle for knowledge. Bjerring's worlds are close to what we think of as worlds containing logical violations. We should note, though, that his impossible worlds can be made sense of only from a classical perspective as consistency plays a crucial role in his characterisation of the alleged impossibility.

[28] See Priest (2005: §1.7).

[29] See Priest (202+).

Ripley (2018) use open worlds as impossible worlds in addition to standard possible worlds to account for the semantics of counterpossibles (counterfactuals with impossible antecedents).[30] Berto & Jago (2019) argue in the context of counterpossibles that

> impossible worlds in general cannot be closed under any logical principle. (p. 176)[31]

Most recently, Priest (202+) writes:

> a possible world is one that is closed under logical consequence, and an impossible world is one that is not. (§1)[32]

He does not intend this to be a definition of impossible worlds. Nevertheless, he takes it to be the 'guiding thought' for understanding impossible worlds. Nolan (2017) also claims in the context of examining causal counterfactuals that

> What is true according to possible worlds is closed under logical consequence, but this is not in general the case for impossible worlds. (pp. 26–27)

So, it is open worlds that often (though not always) play a role in motivating and introducing impossible worlds, although no one seems to define impossible worlds as open worlds.

But, what exactly is it for a world to be open? As we saw above, Berto & Jago (2019), Nolan (2017), and Priest (2005, 202+) define an open world as a world that is not closed under logical consequence. A common conception of what it is for a world to be closed under a logic is in terms of truth preservation; a world is closed under some logic, just in case everything that, according to that logic, follows from what is true at that world is also true at that world. However, if this is how we understand closure and open worlds are characterised as not being closed under *any* logic, there will be no open worlds at which something is true. Given that if A is true at a world, it is true there, a world where something is true must be closed under at least Identity ($A \models A$). Thus, it seems that there cannot be any world that is not closed under *any* logical consequence if we understand closure in terms of truth preservation.

---

[30] See §7 for more on counterpossibles.

[31] It is not clear that Jago is committed to this; see Jago (2007, 2009).

[32] See also Priest (2016b: ch. 9). Given that Priest introduced open worlds in addition to 'impossible worlds', what made him change his mind about the status of open worlds as impossible worlds? That's anyone's guess. However, there is a tight connection between open worlds and logically different worlds (see §6.1).

We can avoid this result in at least two salient ways.[33] One option is to restrict the kind of logical consequence that features in the definition. Instead of defining an open world in terms of the failure of closure under *any* logic, we might define a world to be open if it is not closed under *its own* logic. The other option is to revise our conception of what it is to be closed under logical consequence. Instead of understanding closure in terms of truth preservation, we might understand it in some other way. We will consider these two options in what follows.

4.1 Anarchy

One common way to understand openness follows the 'motto ... that at an impossible world, anything can happen' (Priest (2016b: 190)). Given that the focus here is on *logical* impossibility, following this motto, open worlds are understood as worlds where anything happens with respect to logic. A logic specifies valid inferences and separates them from invalid ones. So, a world where anything happens is a world where logical operations are unsystematic. That is, at an open world, all logical operations behave arbitrarily. An open world understood in this way is, thus, a world where assignments of truth values to atomic *and* complex sentences are all arbitrary. This means that, at an open world, the evaluation of A is independent of that of B for *any* A and B. This is the kind of open worlds popularised by Priest (2005). But it was Rantala (1982a, 1982b) who first introduced them to address the problem of logical ominiscience in the context of epistemic logic. Let's call worlds of this kind *Rantala worlds* and see Rantala worlds in action.[34]

Consider a *Rantala frame* which is a structure $\langle W, N, R \rangle$ where W is the set of worlds, $N \subseteq W$ is the set of normal worlds (then, $W - N$ is the set of Rantala worlds) and $R \subseteq W \times W$ is a binary relation on worlds. Once a Rantala frame is equipped with an evaluation function, we have a *Rantala model* $\langle W, N, R, v \rangle$. At normal worlds, atomic sentences are assigned truth values by the evaluation function and complex sentences are evaluated recursively in the standard manner. However, at a Rantala world, *all* sentences, whether atomic or complex, are assigned a truth value by the evaluation function directly. This allows an evaluation of p to be independent of that of $p \vee q$, for instance. So, $p \vee q$ may be non-true even if p is true. Then, to generate a logic using Rantala models, validity is defined in terms of truth-preservation at all normal worlds in all Rantala models.

---

[33] Presumably for the reason given above, Berto & Jago (2019) define an open world as a world which is 'not closed under any consequence relation other than *identity*, $A \models A$' (p. 113).

[34] The presentation of Rantala worlds here follows that of Berto & Jago (2019: §5.3).

As we saw before, open worlds were introduced to reject various closure principles such as the closure principle for a knowledge operator K:

If KA and $A \models B$, then KB.

In order to reject this, one can provide the following counter-model within a Rantala frame that is modified to apply to epistemic context:

$$w_1 \longrightarrow w_2$$
$$p$$

Figure 1

where $N = \{w_1\}$ (Berto & Jago (2019: 113)) as in Figure 1. (If a sentence, whether atomic or complex, does not appear in the graphic representation of the model, it is non-true.) Since p is true at w_2, Kp is true at w_1 (where K works just like $\Box$). Also, given that validity is defined in terms of truth preservation at all normal worlds, $p \models p \vee q$. But $p \vee q$ is non-true at w_2. So $K(p \vee q)$ is non-true at w_1. Hence the closure principle in question is invalidated.

One way to describe a Rantala world (or worlds introduced to invalidate various closure principles) is that it is logically *anarchic* (Berto & Jago (2019: §5.4)). At a Rantala world, all sentences, whether atomic or complex, are assigned truth values by the evaluation function directly. This means that complex sentences are evaluated just like atomic sentences. A consequence of this is that logical operations are not recursive. In fact, there is nothing systematic about any of the logical operators. For instance, the evaluation of $p \vee q$ is independent of that of p. So, at a Rantala world, there is no systematic relationship between $p \vee q$ and p.

Now, anarchy is something that holds *at* (or *in*) a world or worlds. If an assignment of truth values is arbitrary, it is at a world that logical operations are arbitrary. In other words, it is the logical operations *intrinsic* to a world that are anarchic.[35] This means that an anarchic world is open in a restrictive sense: an anarchic world is open when the world is not closed under any *intrinsic* logic (a logic that holds at that world).

4.2 Nihilism

Another class of worlds that might be regarded as open are logically nihilistic worlds. Logically nihilistic worlds are worlds at which no logic holds. Using our terminology, this means that there are no entailment schemas that hold at (or in) that world. If a world is logically nihilistic in this way, there is no logic

---

[35] This way of describing these logical operations as intrinsic can be found in Priest (202+).

intrinsic to the world. So a logically nihilistic world is open because there is no logic intrinsic to the world under which the world is closed. Given that there is no logic that holds at (or in) a logically nihilistic world, there is no internal perspective from which to close the world. Thus, a logically nihilistic world is an open world. (Depending on how to define closure, a logically nihilistic world may also be closed because it is closed under *any* logic, assuming that we allow 'any logic' to be satisfied vacuously.[36] But the focus here is on openness.)

4.3 Silence

Anarchy and nihilism are notions of openness that concern logics that hold at worlds. It restricts which logics are in play when characterising openness. There is, however, a way to understand the notion of openness that is non-restrictive but which does not fall into the trap of implying that there are no open worlds at which something is true. The idea is to appeal to *silent worlds* (Tanaka (202+)).

Let's assume that p and q are propositions that are part of the language and $A \models B$ (where A and B are meta-variables) is an entailment schema that expresses a law of logic. $A \models B$ does not have to be intrinsic to a silent world: it may be an entailment schema that holds at the actual world but does not hold at the silent world, for instance. For p and q, however, we assume that they represent facts that obtain at a world. There may be some p and q such that $\models$ is *undefined* for them at a world. This is the case when there is no logical relation between p and q according to $\models$. In such a case, we say that $\models$ is *silent* about p and q at the world. Then, a world w is silent if there are some propositions of the language, p and q, representing facts obtaining at w such that $\models$ is silent about them.

A silent world is like a *situation* which is incomplete with respect to the assignments of truth values (Barwise (1989), Barwise & Perry (1983)). For instance, the political situation in Australia does not say anything about the political situation in New Zealand. The truth value of the proposition expressing the political situation in New Zealand is undefined in a political situation in Australia. In this respect, a situation is silent about the truth values of some propositions. However, there is an important difference between a situation and a silent world. In a situation, it is the assignment of truth values of propositions that is undefined; whereas, in a silent world, it is the consequence relation between propositions that is undefined. This difference becomes important in considering *logical* impossibility.

---

[36] Thanks go to an anonymous reviewer for pointing this out.

In order to describe a silent world as an open world, we have to reexamine the notion of closure that often plays a crucial role in defining open worlds. When we questioned the cogency of characterising openness as amounting to not being closed under logical consequence, we used a semantic consideration. We claimed that if A is true at a world, it must be true there; and so Identity ($A \models A$) must hold. To then think that a world must be closed at least under Identity is to think of closure to be a semantic matter. However, the notion of closure does not have to be semantic. We might understand it in terms of the laws of logic subsuming their instances. Let S be a set of entailment schemas representing the laws of logic that hold at a world. Then, we might think that a world is closed under S if all the instances $s \in S$ are subsumed by S at the world.

Now, let's assume that $A \models B$ is an entailment schema. If a world w is silent with respect to p and q, then neither $p \models q$ nor $p \not\models q$ holds at w. However, $p \models q$ is an instance of $A \models B$. So $A \models B$ does not subsume some of its instances at w. Thus, if a world is silent with respect to *any* entailment schema, then a silent world is not closed and, hence, it is an open world. The notion of openness appealed to here is unrestrictive as a silent world is open when it is silent with respect to any entailment schema.

Just like we distinguished silent worlds from situations, we must also distinguish silent worlds from what we might call logically nihilistic worlds. A logically nihilistic world is a world where no logic holds. In our terminology, this means that it is a world where the set of entailment schemas that hold at the world is empty. The set of entailment schemas that hold at a silent world does not have to be empty, however. At a silent world, a logical law may hold even though it may fail to subsume some or all of its instances. This feature of a silent world will be important in considering such a world as an impossible world as we see below.

4.4 Openness as Impossibility?

Before examining whether or not anarchic worlds, logically nihilistic worlds and silent worlds should count as impossible worlds, we should note that there is a *prima facie* reason to think that openness as such cannot be the mark of impossibility. Identifying openness as the mark of impossibility sometimes comes with identifying closure as the mark of possibility as Priest (202+) does explicitly. However, closure appears not to be the mark of possibility. Consider a *trivial world*, w_T, at which everything (every sentence or well-formed formula of the language) is true. To be more precise, let L be a set of propositional language consisting of atomic sentences ($p, q, \ldots$) and well-formed formulas consisting of atomic sentences and logical operators ($\neg$, $\wedge$, $\vee$). Then, at w_T, for any $A \in L$, A is evaluated as true. Since everything is true at w_T, reasoning in accordance with any law of logic leads from truth to truth. So w_T is closed under any logic. Thus, if closure is the mark of possibility, a trivial world, w_T, comes out as possible.[37] However, a trivial world seems and is widely thought to be *impossible*. For instance, Nolan (1997: 544) suggests that a world where everything is true is 'one of the most absurd situations conceivable' and Weber & Omori (2019: 976) call such a world 'the *ultimate* impossibility'. If the trivial world is impossible, closure cannot be the mark of possibility. If defining impossible worlds in terms of openness is paired with defining possible worlds in terms of closure, there is *prima facie* reason to think that openness is not the defining characteristic of impossible worlds. So, how can we understand open worlds so that openness might be taken to be indicative of impossibility?

4.5 Anarchy as Impossibility?

An anarchic world is a world at which logical operations are unsystematic. It is an open world in the sense that it is not closed under any logic intrinsic to the anarchic world. Having clarified the sense in which an anarchic world is open, we can now work out how an anarchic world might be thought of as characteristially impossible. We will argue that anarchy is not sufficient nor necessary for a world to be impossible.

First, logical anarchy cannot be sufficient for impossibility. This is because an anarchic world *is* closed under an anarchic logic according to which $A \models B$ holds for any A and B. This is the case even though it is not plausible to think that such a logic is 'correct', that is, it is not plausible that it is the actual logic.[38] This means that openness cannot be sufficient for the impossibility of a world.

Second, logical anarchy isn't necessary for impossibility. Consider a world which we call a *Mortensen world*. At a Mortensen world, everything is possible (Mortensen (1989)). Given that everything is possible, arbitrary assignments of truth values to atomic and complex sentences must also be possible at a Mortensen world. So, *if* a Mortensen world is possible, an anarchic world is possible. Hence, an anarchic world is not necessarily an impossible world as it may be possible.

---

[37] In fact, Priest (202+: §4) admits that a trivial world comes out as possible according to the semantics he provides.

[38] See, however, Estrada-González (2012) and Kabay (2010) who defend trivialism. In the way that they understand the matter, it is the consequence relation rather than a world (or a theory) that is trivial. Thus, what they call a trivial logic is an anarchic logic in our sense. In order to avoid any confusion, we call it an anarchic logic.

Perhaps, however, anarchic worlds are impossible relative to the actual world. Except Mortensen, very few think that everything is actually possible. Moreover, it might be thought that closure is a special property of the actual world. That is, the actual world might best be understood as closed such that all the worlds that are actually possible are also closed. In this case, an anarchic world might be thought to be impossible relative to the actual world. This line of thought assumes that an anarchic world is different from the actual world. So, it does not seem to be anarchy that is making for the impossibility of these worlds; rather, it is difference. Moreover, this line of thought relies on the actual world that is *extrinsic* to the anarchic world in question. Hence, there does not seem to be anything about a world's being anarchic that, in itself, is a necessary condition on its being impossible.

Lastly, if there is anything impossible about a logically anarchic world, that seems to be because it contains counterexamples to some set of logical laws. In the next section, we will describe such a world as a world containing logical *violations*. For now, we will show that a logically anarchic world contains counterexamples to some laws of logic.

Recall that, at a logically anarchic world, the evaluation of $p \vee q$ is independent of that of p. So, $p \vee q$ may be non-true even though p (or q) is true. However, at a non-anarchic, normal world, the evaluation of $p \vee q$ may depend on the evaluations of p (and q). At least, this is the case in a Rantala model. Given that validity is defined in terms of truth-preservation at all normal worlds in all (Rantala) models, Disjunction Introduction ($A \models A \vee B$) may be valid (though this depends on how disjunction behaves at normal worlds). This example shows that what is characteristic of logically anarchic worlds is that they contain counterexamples. The characteristic feature of a logically anarchic world is not that it is open but that it contains counterexamples. Thus, if there is anything impossible about a logically anarchic world, that is because it contains counterexamples to the logical laws that hold at the world.

4.6 Nihilism as Impossibility?

Is there any reason to think that an open world understood as logically nihilistic world is impossible? There seems to be a reason to think that a logically nihilistic world is possible (although this does not necessarily rule out such a world being impossible as well). Logical nihilism is often motivated in the context of the debate between logical monism and logical pluralism. Logical monism is the view that there is only one 'correct' logic and logical pluralism is the view that there are at least two 'correct' or 'admissible' logics.[39] If logical pluralism

---

[39] For logical monism, see Priest (2001). There are more work done on logical pluralism, for instance, see Beall & Restall (2006), Lynch (2009), and Russell (2008).

is a possible view, then, even if it turns out to be false, it raises the possibility that the number of 'correct' or 'admissible' logics could not only go up from one but could also go down, that is, down to zero. So, logical pluralism seems to make it possible that there is no logic. In other words, logical pluralism, if it is a possible view, leads to the possibility of logical nihilism.[40] If this line of argument works, a logically nihilistic world is possible. Hence, it is not clear that an open world understood as a logically nihilistic world should necessarily count as impossible.

4.7 Silence as Impossibility?

Characterising anarchy as the mark of impossibility seems to face difficulty as we saw above. What about silent worlds? Is there a sense in which silent worlds should count as impossible?

To answer this question, consider LHS: the laws of logic that hold at a world supervene on their instances at that world. One important feature of a silent world is that LHS fails with respect to a set of logical laws. At a silent world, $p \models q$ may not hold for some p and q even if $A \models B$ holds. Because the world may be silent about $p \models q$ (and $p \not\models q$), the instances of the law $A \models B$, for instance, $p \models q$, may not cooperate with the law. Hence, LHS does not necessarily hold.

Interestingly, however, this does not mean that there are counterexamples to the laws of logic within that world. When we introduced LHS, we characterised its failure in terms of the existence of counterexamples to a set of laws. At a silent world, however, that is not how LHS fails. That the world does not say anything about the consequence relation between p and q does not mean that $p \models q$ takes you from a good value to a bad value. So, LHS fails not because there are counterexamples to a set of logical laws but because a silent world is silent about the instances of the laws.

Regardless of how it fails, the failure of LHS might be thought to point towards impossibility. If LHS fails, there are instances of the laws of logic that do not accord the laws. This is the case even though there are no counterexamples and, thus, there are no instances that go *against* the laws. However, it might be thought that the laws of logic subsume their instances by the very nature of the laws. So, there is a sense in which, from the point of view of the laws, it is impossible for the instances of the laws to not align with the laws.

---

[40] See Russell (2017). For more detailed arguments for logical nihilism, see Cotnoir (2018) and Russell (2018).

If a silent world is impossible, that is because some instances of the laws of logic come apart from the laws.[41]

5 Violation

The last characteristic of impossible worlds we explore in this Element is something that, until recently, did not receive much explicit attention and, when it was mentioned, it was discussed in passing and the discussion moved quickly to difference or openness. Despite this, it is this characteristic that is often used to motivate the very idea of (logical) impossibility. That is the notion of *logical violation*.

A logical violation can be defined as follows. Suppose that an entailment schema of the form $A \models B$ holds at a world w. As was defined in Conceptual Prolegomenon, *counterexamples* to an entailment schema $A_1, A_2, \ldots \models B_1, B_2, \ldots$ at a world w are $p_1, p_2, \ldots$ and $q_1, q_2, \ldots$ that hold at w such that p_i and q_i can be used to instantiate $A_1, A_2, \ldots \models B_1, B_2, \ldots$ where all the premises are true and the conclusions non-true. Then, a law of logic is *violated* at w if the entailment schema that expresses that logical law has a counterexample at w.

An impossible world can then be characterised as a world that contains at least one logical violation. According to this definition, at an impossible world, at least one logical law is violated. The idea captured by logical violation is that, from the point of view of the logical laws, counterexamples are impossible given that a logical law subsumes all its instances. Thus, a world is impossible relative to some set of laws if some instance of a logical law violates that law at that world.

5.1 Non-normal Worlds

Non-normal worlds were introduced to capture the semantics for non-normal modal logics such as *S2* and *S3* as well as various relevant logics (see §2.2). In the literature on impossible worlds, they are often appealed to in motivating and demystifying impossible worlds. A non-normal world is a world where $\Box A$ is non-true even if A is true at all worlds ($\models A$) and, thus, $\Box A$ is true at all worlds ($\models \Box A$) or a world where $B \to B$ is non-true even if it is a logical truth ($\models B \to B$). This feature of non-normal worlds has been glossed as worlds where the laws of logic fail. For instance, Priest (1992) describes non-normal worlds as follows:

> non-normal worlds are essentially those where theorems, that is, semantically, logical truths may fail. (p. 292)

---

[41] See Tanaka (202+).

If we take a logical truth to express a law of logic, a non-normal world is described as a world where a law of logic may fail. This observation about non-normal worlds has then been developed in terms of logical difference (Priest (1992, 2008, 202+)) or openness (Berto & Jago (2019)).

However, it is not clear that the above analysis provides an adequate description of non-normal worlds. It is misleading to say that the laws of logic may fail at a non-normal world. We can see this clearly in the case of relevant logics. In (most) relevant logics, $B \to B$ is a logical truth (and, thus, expresses a law of logic) even in the presence of a non-normal world where $B \to B$ is non-true. So it is not quite correct to say that 'logical truths [the laws of logic] may fail' (Berto & Jago (2019)).

Instead, what goes on at a non-normal world is that it may provide a counterexample to a law of logic. In the case of relevant logic, at a non-normal world, for some p, $p \to p$ may be non-true. But this does not necessarily invalidate $B \to B$ as it is a law of logic. Nevertheless, if $p \to p$ is non-true, such p serves as a counterexample to the logical law $B \to B$. So the law of logic does not fail but it is *violated*. What happens at a non-normal world is, thus, that a law of logic may be violated. Hence, a non-normal world is a world that may contain logical violations of some logical laws.

5.2 How Do Violations Account for Impossibility?

A world that contains logical violations has distinctive features that are absent from logically different worlds and open worlds. In this section, we will examine three such features. Articulating those features illuminate how logical violations account for impossibility.

5.2.1 Impossibility Is Relative

A violation is a violation of some set of laws. A world may contain a violation of one set of laws but may not contain any violations of a different set of laws. For instance, consider two worlds, w_1 and w_2, where classical logic holds at w_1 while a paraconsistent logic holds at w_2. In particular, *ex contradictione quodlibet* (ECQ): $A, \neg A \models B$, is valid at w_1 but invalid at w_2. Suppose further that, at a third world w_3, there is a true contradiction (for some p, p is both true and non-true) but not everything is true. In such a case, w_3 *violates* some laws of logic that hold at w_1. Any p which is both true and non-true and q which is (just) non-true are counterexamples to ECQ at w_3. However, w_3 may not violate any laws of logic that hold at w_2. So, if we characterise impossibility in terms of violations, w_3 is impossible relative to the laws that hold at w_1; however, it is not impossible relative to the laws that hold at w_2. If we describe impossibility in terms of violations, thus, impossibility can only be understood as relative and cannot be understood in any absolute sense.

5.2.2 Impossibility Violates LHS

A world contains a logical violation if it contains a counterexample to a set of logical laws. If it contains counterexamples, there are instances of the logical laws that are non-true at that world. This means that the logical laws (expressed by the entailment schemas) and the (non-logical) facts (at least, their logical qualities) can come apart at a world that contains logical violations, in particular, when the laws that hold at a world are violated at that same world.

To see how logical laws get separated from facts, let's go back to the analogy to physical laws that we examined in the context of logical difference. In the analogy, there being a stable 101 kg lump of gold is described as impossible in a world where the laws of physics are different from the actual world and as possible (even though it is contingently non-true) in the actual world. But why is it impossible that there be a stable 101 kg lump of gold in the physically different world?

The world in question is a world where there is a law to the effect that all lumps of gold more than or equal to 100 kg explode. In such a world, there could *not* be a stable 101 kg lump of gold since such a lump would spontaneously explode as dictated by the law. And the reason why there could not be such a lump of gold is because the existence of such a lump would violate the laws of physics that hold in that world. Hence, what accounts for the impossibility of the existence of a stable 101 kg lump of gold in the world with the law in question and the possibility of it in the actual world is the fact that the existence of the lump violates the laws that hold in the former but not those that hold in the later. So what makes the world with the law impossible is the fact that the existence of the lump of gold serves as a counterexample to the law at the world.

Now, LHS states that the laws of logic supervenes on their instances. But, if the world contains a logical violation of the laws that hold at that world, the laws and facts may come apart. So, at a world that contains logical violations of its own laws, LHS may fail to hold. Hence, LHS may not hold if there are impossible worlds that contain logical violations.

5.2.3 Impossibility Is Something That Happens

As the failure of LHS indicates, an impossible world, under the characterisation in terms of logical violations, is a world where impossibility happens. The notion of violations concerns not only logical laws but also (non-logical) facts as the presence of counterexamples can reveal discrepancies between the laws and facts. So, impossibility is not always a matter of logical laws being somehow impossible. Impossibility, if we understand it in terms of violations, is not given by the structure of the logical space. Rather, it is something that happens at a world (Tanaka (202+)).

However, what counts as impossible is relative to a set of logical laws. So, the question of whether a world is impossible or not has no fixed answer, since the answer depends on a set of logical laws with respect to which we are characterising the world. Thus, if we understand impossibility in terms of the presence of logical violations, we shouldn't think of impossible worlds as the worlds that need to be *added* to the set of all worlds in the way that Priest (2005) conceives of them as is shown by Figure 2 (Priest (2005: 22, Figure 1.1)):[42]

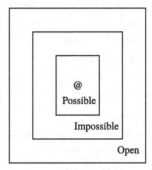

Figure 2

where, in Priest's terminology, impossible worlds are the non-normal worlds that are used for the semantics for non-normal modal systems and for the semantics for relevant logics, and possible and impossible worlds are considered to be closed.[43] Instead, logical violations allow us to understand impossible worlds as worlds that are already there when all the worlds are delivered by the comprehension principle for worlds, which are then categorised as possible or impossible with respect to this or that set of laws of logic.

5.2.4 Impossibility Is Contingent

In characterising impossibility in terms of violations, impossibility is characterised as something that happens at a world rather than as an aspect of some set of logical laws. Impossibility is accounted for not only by the properties that

---

[42] Labels have been modified for explicit labelling.

[43] Priest (202+) claims that the non-normal worlds for relevant logics must be closed because *modus ponens* holds at those worlds.

some logical laws may possess but also by the (non-logical) facts that obtain at some world. So, what counts as impossible if we are to think of impossibility in terms of violation is a contingent matter. Hence, in characterising impossibility in terms of violations, we are not concerned with identifying a fixed region of logical space that is carved out by the logical laws; rather, we are concerned with the contingent features of the worlds.

In claiming that impossibility is a contingent matter, it should be noted that the failure of LHS is also a contingent matter.[44] For instance, it may be contingent on the condition under which the logical laws hold at the actual world. There are at least three ways in which the actual laws might hold as described below. The failure of LHS may be contingent on those ways in which the actual laws are conceived to hold.

First, the actual laws might be *tolerant*. A set of laws is tolerant just in case, given those laws, it is possible that the laws are strictly weaker or strictly stronger than they actually are. We considered such laws in relation to difference. In an analogy to the physical laws, we considered different sets of physical laws (and, analogously, different sets of logical laws). If such an analogy is cogent, the physical laws at the actual world do not impede the possibility of them being different. Likewise, the logical laws at the actual world may be tolerant. If the actual laws are indeed tolerant, a set of laws that hold at a world may come apart from the facts that obtain at that world. LHS may then fail. In this case, the failure of LHS is contingent on the actual laws of logic being tolerant.

Second, the actual laws might be *wide open*. A set of laws is wide open if *anything* is possible given those laws. This means that if a set of laws is wide open, it is maximally permissive. If Mortensen (1989) is right that everything is possible, the actual laws of logic are maximally permissive. If the actual laws are wide open in this way, there may be a world where the laws and facts come apart.

Third, the actual laws might be *obstinate*. A set of laws is obstinate if, given those laws, it is impossible that the laws are any weaker or stronger than they actually are. If the actual laws are obstinate, there will be no worlds that are logically different from the worlds that do not contain a violation of the actual laws. When we consider what would be possible, necessary, obligatory, or permissible under certain counterfactual circumstances, the parties to the disputes are often required to imagine what would be possible and what must be

---

[44] By claiming that Humean supervenience – a more general version of Logical Humean Supervenience – holds contingently, D. Lewis (1986) would concur.

impossible (in the relevant sense) if their interlocutors were correct. That is, they are often required to consider *coutermetapossibles* like the following:

1. If paraconsistent logic were the correct logic, it would be possible to validly infer every proposition from a contradiction.
2. If gravity had followed an inverse cube law (rather than an inverse square law), the actual movements of the planets would be impossible.

These are called 'countermetapossibles' because they are concerned with what would be possible and impossible if the actual laws (and not just facts) were different or not even possible.[45] In evaluating a countermetapossible, we need to fix the laws to be as dictated in the antecedent and see whether the consequent also holds at those worlds. In so doing, there is no guarantee that the (non-logical) facts stay the same across all worlds. In fact, if there is a multiplicity of worlds, given that we are assuming the laws to be the same, different sets of facts must hold at different worlds. Then, there may be worlds where facts do not match the laws. In such a case, LHS fails. Again, if it fails, it fails contingent on the actual laws being obstinate.

6 Difference, Openness, and Violation

Now that we have introduced the notions of difference, openness, and violation that have been appealed to in characterising impossible worlds, we can try to understand the relationship between them. We will show that difference, openness and violation are not equivalent to each other. However, we will also show the conditions under which they are equivalent as a way of showing the relationship between them.

6.1 Difference and Openness

A logically different world is a world whose laws of logic are different (especially from those that hold at the actual world). An open world, on the other hand, does not necessarily hold a different set of logical laws from the ones that hold at the actual world. For instance, at a logically anarchic world, the laws of logic may be the same as those that hold at the actual world. It is just that there may be some instances of the laws that do not obey the laws (see §4.5). Hence, difference and openness are not equivalent in the sense that a logically different world and an open world may be two different worlds.

---

[45] Countermetapossibles are a generalisation of countermetalogicals discussed in Sandgren & Tanaka (2020). For more on countermetapossibles and their variations, see §7.

However, Priest (202+: §1) takes it as the 'guiding thought' that 'a possible world is one that is closed under logical consequence and an impossible world is one that is not'. In trying to understand what exactly that thought comes down to, he suggests to think about logical impossibility in analogy with physical impossibility. He then provides an analogy like the ones that we saw in §3 (Priest (202+: §5)). Thus, for Priest, the notions of difference and openness are tightly intertwined.

It is not clear why Priest tightly connects difference and openness since he does not spell it out. However, there are conditions under which difference amounts to openness. As we saw in §4, one way a world is open is for there to be no laws of logic *at* the world, that is, a world is a logically nihilistic world. If a world is logically nihilistic, there are no laws of logic intrinsic to the world under which it can be closed. Hence, such a world is open. But this is one way in which a world is logically different. To see this, we note that logically different worlds are worlds where different sets of logical laws hold *at* those worlds. In the analogy to physical impossibility, it is assumed that a physically different world has the laws of physics (or nature) that hold at or in that world. These laws do not 'spill' over to other worlds: the effects of the laws are all contained within the world. This is why a physically different world may be a world where the physically impossible Olympics may take place. But, any world whose set of the logical laws is different from, for instance, the actual world, no matter how small the difference is, still counts as a logically different world. And, one set of logical laws that is different from, for instance, the set of logical laws holding at the actual world, is an empty one. So, when the set of logical laws that hold at a world is empty, that world is logically different. Hence, an open world may count as logically different world if it is a logically nihilistic world.

6.2 Difference and Violation

Similarly, even though difference is not generally equivalent to violation, there are conditions under which difference counts as a violation. Consider a world w_1 where the laws of logic are classical. At w_1, ECQ is valid ($A, \neg A \models B$ holds at w_1). Now consider another world w_2 where the laws of logic are those of LP (Logic of Paradox, Priest (1979)). So, at w_2, ECQ is invalid ($A, \neg A \models B$ does not hold at w_2). They are, thus, worlds where different logical laws hold. That is, they are *logically different* worlds.

Now, LP is a sub-logic of classical logic in the sense that all of LP theorems are also theorems of classical logic. This means that worlds which contain no violations of classical logic will not contain violations of LP. However, worlds in which LP holds and which contain no violations of LP laws may contain violations of the classical laws. Hence, despite the fact that w_1 (where the classical laws hold) and w_2 (where the laws of LP hold) are logically different, w_1 does not contain violations with respect to w_2 as there are no counterexamples of LP laws at w_1. Thus, logically different worlds do not always contain violations of each other's laws. So, logical difference comes apart from the presence of logical violations.

Despite the fact that difference is not equivalent to violations, there are some situations where difference counts as a violation. We can illustrate the conditions under which difference constitutes violations by providing a schema for a modal semantics that makes room for the distinctions between difference and violation. This will help us see the relationships between difference and violation.

Consider the set of all worlds.[46] We assume unrestricted comprehension principle following Nolan (1997) and Priest (2016a). So, for any set of statements Γ (including entailment schemas), there is at least one world where Γ is true. To this, we introduce an 'accessibility' relation that tracks the absence of violation, *v-accessibility*. We say that w_1 v-accesses w_2 just in case w_2 contains no violations of the laws of logic that hold at w_1. Conversely, if w_1 does not v-access w_2 then w_2 contains at least one violation of the laws of logic that hold at w_1.

Within this schema, we can define logical difference. A world w_1 is logically different from w_2 iff either there is some world that is v-accessible from w_1 that is not v-accessible from w_2 or that is v-accessible from w_2 but not from w_1. For instance, Figure 3

Figure 3

(where the arrows mark v-accessibility) represents a situation where w_1 and w_2 are logically different. That is, logically different worlds v-access different worlds; different things count as logical violations according to logically different worlds. This schema does not provide a complete theory of (logical) impossibility; however, it does allow us to visualise how logical difference relates to violations and in what way logical difference involves violations.[47]

---

[46] These need not be 'worlds' on any strong sense of that term. They can be understood as points of evaluation at which statements are true.

[47] See Sandgren & Tanaka (2020).

6.3 Openness and Violation

If a world is open, it does not necessarily contain a violation. An open world is one that is not closed under logical consequence. There are two ways in which a world can be open while not containing a violation. First, if a world is logically nihilistic and open, there are no laws of logic that hold at that world. Then, there is no set of laws that is violated. Second, if a consequence relation is silent about some propositions that hold at a world, then it does not say anything about the validity between those propositions. So there are no instances of a law of logic involving those propositions that can serve as counterexamples. Hence, if a world is silent about some instances of the logical laws, it does not necessarily contain a violation. Hence, an open world does not necessarily contain a violation. So, in general, openness comes apart from violations.

However, as we have seen, if a world is logically anarchic, it may contain a violation of the logical laws. At a logically anarchic world, the operation of $\vee$, for instance, is not recursive. So $p \vee q$ is evaluated independently of p and q. Then, it may not be that $p \models p \vee q$ as $p \vee q$ may be non-true even if p (or q) is true. This is the case even if $A \models A \vee B$ is a law of logic. In such a case, the instances of the law may come apart from the law. If a world is logically anarchic in this way, it contains counterexamples to the law of logic. Hence, a logically anarchic world may contain violations of the laws of logic.

7 Counterpossibles and Countermetapossibles

In the second half of this Element, we consider various theoretical roles that impossible worlds are introduced to play. The most obvious applications of impossible worlds are counterfactuals. A counterfactual is a conditional whose antecedent may not be factual. That is, the antecedent of a counterfactual may not be true at the actual world even when the counterfactual is true at the actual world. One way to evaluate a counterfactual is then to invoke possible worlds, ways things could be. However, there may be a counterfactual whose antecedent is not just actually non-true but impossible. Perhaps, such a conditional should be treated as trivially true (Kratzer (1977), D. Lewis (1973), Stalnaker (1968)). However, making sense of such a conditional in order to evaluate it requires non-trivially representing impossible situations and impossible worlds are a natural tool for representing situations in which the impossible antecedent is true.

In this section, we will survey the variations of counterfactuals whose antecedents are impossible. We will use the distinctions between difference, openness and violation that we introduced and examined in Sections 3–6 as the framework to analyse various kinds of counterfactuals. In so doing, we will shed new light on the features and utility of impossible worlds that have been introduced to do various tasks.

7.1 Counterpossibles

A *counterpossible* is a kind of counterfactual conditional whose antecedent involves impossibility. The following conditionals are often-cited examples of counterpossibles (Nolan (1997)):

(1) If Hobbes had (secretly) squared the circle, all sick children in the mountains of South America at the time would have cared.
(2) If Hobbes had (secretly) squared the circle, all sick children in the mountains of South America at the time would not have cared.

Given that it is impossible to square a circle, these conditionals have impossible antecedents and they are, thus, counterpossibles.

The standard semantics for counterfactuals of Kratzer (1977), D. Lewis (1973) and Stalnaker (1968) evaluate both of the above counterpossibles as true. According to that semantics, a counterfactual is true iff the consequent is true at all possible worlds closest to the actual world satisfying the antecedent. But if a counterfactual has an impossible antecedent, there is no possible world where the antecedent is true. So if we apply this semantics for counterfactuals to evaluate the above counterpossibles, they are both *vacuously* true.

Whatever the 'intuition' one may have about the sick children in the mountains of South America, evaluating both counterpossibles to come out true looks implausible.[48] The consequents of those counterpossibles are contradictory. So it is hard to make sense of treating them as logically equivalent.

The easiest way to accommodate this line of thought is to supplement the possible world based semantics for counterfactuals with impossible worlds.[49] Then, since there may be a world, that is, an impossible world, where the antecedent is true, the evaluation of a counterpossible is *nonvacuous*. The truth value of the conditional depends on the truth value of the consequent at the closest worlds to the actual world where the antecedent is true.

A simple nonvacuist semantics for counterpossibles can be presented as follows (adapted from Berto et al. (2018)). Given a propositional language including connectives ¬, ∧, ∨, □→ (the counterfactual conditional) and modal

---

[48] See, however, T. Williamson (2020: ch. 15, 2021) who argues that the 'intuitive' impulse to evaluate counterpossibles such as (1) and (2) *nonvacuously* is misguided: 'instincts are not always to be trusted' (T. Williamson (2020: 259)). For more on this, see §8.

[49] It is possible to analyse counterpossibles without using impossible worlds. See French, Girard, & Ripley (2022).

operators □ and ◇, let Π be the set of propositional parameters and Φ be the set of formulas. An interpretation is a tuple $\langle W, P, R_A, v \rangle$ where

- W is the set of all worlds, possible and impossible
- $P \subset W$ is the set of possible worlds (and $I = W - P$ is the set of impossible worlds)
- $R_A \subset W \times W$ is a binary relation on W for every $A \in \Phi$
- v is an evaluation function

R_A can be understood in terms of the closest world in which A is true. The notion of closeness or similarity is not required to be any different from the standard account except that impossible worlds have to be part of the closeness or similarity relations.

The evaluation function, v, assigns 1 or 0 to every propositional parameter $p \in \Pi$ at every $w \in W$ ($v_w(p) = 1$ or $v_w(p) = 0$) and to every formula $A \in \Phi$ at every *impossible* world ($v_w(A) = 1$ or $v_w(A) = 0$). This means that, at an impossible world, v assigns 1 or 0 directly to every formula. The truth conditions for formulas at a possible world, $w \in P$, are standard:

- $v_w(\neg A) = 1$ iff $v_w(A) = 0$ (or it is not the case that $v_w(A) = 1$)
- $v_w(A \wedge B) = 1$ iff $v_w(A) = 1$ and $v_w(B) = 1$
- $v_w(A \vee B) = 1$ iff $v_w(A) = 1$ or $v_w(B) = 1$
- $v_w(\Box A) = 1$ iff for every $w' \in P$, $v_{w'}(A) = 1$
- $v_w(\Diamond A) = 1$ iff for some $w' \in P$, $v_{w'}(A) = 1$
- $v_w(A \Box\!\!\rightarrow B) = 1$ iff for every $w' \in W$ such that $R_A w w'$, $v_{w'}(B) = 1$

Validity is defined in terms of truth-preservation at all *possible* worlds of all interpretations:

> $\Sigma \models A$ iff for every interpretation and for every $w \in P$, if $v_w(B) = 1$ for every $B \in \Sigma$, then $v_w(A) = 1$.

This provides a basic nonvacuist account of counterpossibles. As usual, stronger systems can be obtained by adding various constraints on R_A.

In this account, the extensional connectives behave classically and validity is defined in terms of truth-preservation at all *possible* worlds. So, impossible worlds do not play any role in validity. This means that the nonvacuist account presented above behaves just like the standard vacuist account of standard counterfactuals in most cases. A difference between the two is the evaluation of counterpossibles. Consider (1) and (2). There may be an impossible world where Hobbes has squared the circle. So there may be a world where the antecedents of (1) and (2) are true. Such a world may not be contradictory concerning all sick children in the mountains of South America caring about Hobbes' accomplishment. So the truth values of (1) and (2) may come apart. If one's 'intuition' is such that either (1) or (2) is false, then this nonvacuist account can accommodate it.

In order to understand the kind of impossible worlds appealed to in this non-vacuist account of counterpossibles, recall that, at an impossible world, the evaluation function, v, assigns a truth value directly to every formula. So, the standard logical relation between p and $p \vee q$ is lost at some impossible world. Given that p and $p \vee q$ are different formulas, v assigns a truth value to them individually. It may be that p is true while $p \vee q$ is not. Hence, logical operations are anarchic at an impossible world. An impossible world used in the nonvacuist account of counterpossibles presented above is, thus, an open world.

We will see that other kinds of impossible worlds have been used to account for the variations of counterpossibles. We will see that the accounts of *counter-logicals* and *countermathematicals* proposed in the literature can be analysed as appealing to impossible worlds understood as logically or mathematically different worlds or worlds that violate the logical or mathematical laws. Before we examine these accounts, however, it is important to investigate how open worlds as impossible worlds are used in the nonvacuist account of counter-possibles. Such an investigation illuminates how impossible worlds *aka.* open worlds are understood.

In order to emphasise that their nonacuist account of counterpossibles can 'recapture' everything or almost everything that a classical vacuist account of counterfactuals demands, Berto et al. (2018) assume what Nolan (1997) calls the *Strangeness of Impossibility Condition* (SIC):

> *Strangeness of Impossibility Condition:* Any possible world is more similar (or closer) to the actual world than any impossible world. (Nolan (1997: 550))

For instance, consider the following closure principle:

> *Closure:* If $\models (B_1 \wedge \ldots \wedge B_n) \supset C$ then $\models ((A \:\square\!\!\rightarrow B_1) \wedge \ldots \wedge (A \:\square\!\!\rightarrow B_n)) \supset (A \:\square\!\!\rightarrow C)$

where $\supset$ is material conditional. This principle is part of Lewis' system of counterfactuals but it fails in the nonvacuist account of counterpossibles. To see this, notice that an instance of *Closure* is: If $\models B \supset C$ then $\models (A \:\square\!\!\rightarrow B) \supset (A \:\square\!\!\rightarrow C)$. Classically, since $\models (p \wedge \neg p) \supset (q \wedge \neg q)$, $\models (A \:\square\!\!\rightarrow (p \wedge \neg p)) \supset (A \:\square\!\!\rightarrow (q \wedge \neg q))$. If A is $p \wedge \neg p$, by *Reflexivity* of the counterfactual conditional ($\models A \:\square\!\!\rightarrow A$), we can detach the antecedent of the material conditional to get $\models (p \wedge \neg p) \:\square\!\!\rightarrow$

$(q \wedge \neg q)$. Classically, thus, *Closure* (with *Reflexivity* and detachment) entails that a contradiction counterfactually explodes. Given that a nonvacuist account of counterpossibles is developed to prevent such an explosion, *Closure* has to fail in such an account.[50]

However, if we assume SIC, the following closure principle holds:

P-Closure: If $\models (B_1 \wedge \ldots \wedge B_n) \supset C$ then $\Diamond A \models ((A \mathbin{\square\!\!\rightarrow} B_1) \wedge \ldots \wedge (A \mathbin{\square\!\!\rightarrow} B_n)) \supset (A \mathbin{\square\!\!\rightarrow} C)$

That is, if we assume that a certain claim is possible, by SIC, we can focus on the possible worlds and basically ignore all the impossible worlds. Thus, we can recapture the classical principle *Closure* with a classically innocuous suppressed premise $\Diamond A$.

We can see that 'classical recapture' requires SIC, which forces a nonvacuous account of counterpossibles to consider only the possible worlds unless the actual world is actually impossible. However, there are reasons to reject SIC. Most, if not all, reasons given for rejecting SIC in the literature are metaphysical in nature. For instance, consider the impossible omissive claim (Bernstein (2016: 2580)):

The mathematician failed to prove that $2 + 2 = 5$.

Proving that $2 + 2 = 5$ is impossible.[51] However, in the context of proving a mathematical truth about $2 + 2$, the impossible event of the mathematician proving that $2 + 2 = 5$ is more similar (or closer) to the actual event of proving that $2 + 2 = 4$ than the possible event of a random AFL (Aussie Rule) game in which the mathematician did not participate, especially if proving that $2 + 2 = 4$ is tantamount to failing to prove that $2 + 2 = 5$.[52]

There are also reasons to reject SIC that are related to how to conceive of an impossible world. If impossibility (and possibility) is (are) a contingent matter, which world count as impossible can be answered only relative to a world (or a set of logical laws) and the answer cannot be absolute (in the sense of §2.1). In order to evaluate a counterfactual, given a set of worlds, we might order them in terms of similarity. If impossibility is contingent (in the sense appealed to in this Element), the ordering does not determine which world is impossible as what counts as impossible is determined not necessarily in terms of the actual

---

[50] See Berto et al. (2018: 699). *Closure* and the classical account of counterfactuals are defended by Williamson (2007, 2010).

[51] In what sense is this impossible? We will get to this question in §7.3.

[52] See also Nolan (1997: 550f and 569, 2017: 17) for other examples.

world but in terms of a world whether actual or not. In such a case, impossibility is not necessarily a matter of similarity to the actual world as the actual world does not play a privileged role in determining which world counts as impossible. So if impossibility is a contingent matter, SIC does not hold. When we consider variations of counterpossibles, we can see how this plays out. In the next few sections, we will consider *counterlogicals, countermathematicals, countermetapossibles* (of various kinds) and *causal counterfactuals* to examine other ways to understand the involvement of impossible worlds.

7.2 Counterlogicals

A *counterlogical* is a kind of a counterpossible whose antecedent involves logical impossibility. Examples used to illustrate counterlogicals are the following:

> If I had found Sylvan's Box which is and is not empty, I would have made a space ship and sent it into orbit. (Priest (1997b))

> If Saul Kripke were both human and not human, then he would have won the 2000 election. (Goodman (2004))

Both examples have contradictory antecedents which are taken to be logically impossible. They are taken to be counterlogicals under the assumption that classical logic holds at the actual world. But, why are the contradictory antecedents logically impossible?

While the literature is strangely silent on this question (though the literature on counterlogicals is rather small), there are two ways to understand the logical impossibility involved in the above counterlogicals. First, according to classical logic, the Law of Non-Contradiction (LNC) ($\models \neg(A \wedge \neg A)$) holds. If Saul Kripke is and is not human, then there is an instance of A, say p, such that $p \wedge \neg p$ is true (and non-true). So $\neg(p \wedge \neg p)$ is non-true. Hence, there is a counterexample to LNC at a world where the antecedent is true. In this way, the antecedents of the above counterlogicals are impossible in the sense that they *violate* a law of classical logic.[53]

Second, one might think that if there is a counterexample to LNC, LNC must be invalid. So, in order to evaluate a counterlogical nonvacuously, we might invoke a world where a different set of logical laws hold. If a paraconsistent logic holds at such a world, the consequent of a counterlogical may not hold there. For instance, if Sylvan's Box is and is not empty at a world, it may not be that someone who finds it makes a space ship and sends it into orbit, as Priest

---

[53] This seems to be the way that Goodman (2004) understands counterlogicals.

(1997b) urges us to think, in which case the counterlogical might be thought to be not true. If this is the way to understand a counterlogical, then it is a logically different world that is specified in the antecedents.

If we are to think that the impossibility involved in counterlogicals is (logical) difference, a counterlogical seems to become not a species of counterpossibles specifically but of counterfactuals. Counterfactuals have antecedents which may not hold at the actual world. But counterfactuals needn't have impossible antecedents. To identify a contradictory world as a logically different world is to consider a set of logical laws that may not hold at the actual world. But, just like the case of a counterfactual, there is no reason to think that any impossibility plays a role. So, if we understand a counterlogical to involve logically different worlds, there does not need to be anything counter*possible* about counterlogicals.

7.3 Countermathematicals

While counterlogicals have not received much attention, their cousins *countermathematicals* have, at least more attention than counterlogicals. An example of countermathematicals is the following:

> If 13 and 17 weren't each coprime with both 2 and 3, two kinds of subspecies of North American periodical cicada's life cycles would not be 13 and 17. (Baron, Colyvan, & Ripley (2017))

There are two sub-species of North American periodical cicadas. One has a life cycle of 13 years and the other has a life cycle of 17 years (Baker (2005)). By appealing to the countermathematicals such as above, it has been argued that the mathematical facts about 13 and 17 being prime numbers (partly) explain the lengths of their life cycles. Countermathematicals such as above have been used in such arguments.[54]

Our interest here is not with the issue of mathematical explanation that countermathematicals are put to use. Instead, our focus is on the countermathematicals that are made use of in the context of discussing the notion of explanation. There are at least two ways to analyse countermathematicals that do not seem to have been widely recognised in the relevant literature. We will present an analysis of countermathematicals and leave their import to the field of explanation for others to work out.

It has been proposed that there are three steps involved in evaluating a countermathematical (Baron (2020: §3), Baron, Colyvan, & Ripley ((2017: §2), (2020: §2))):

---

[54] Baker (2009, 2017a, 2017b), Baker & Colyvan (2011), Baron (2020), and Baron, Colyvan, & Ripley (2017).

1. *Holding fixed:* Fix some set of facts by choosing them to be invariant under counterfactual variation.
2. *Twiddling:* Twiddle mathematics to make the antecedent of a countermathematical true.
3. *Ramifying:* Consider the ramification of twiddling the facts that are not fixed.

To evaluate the above countermathematical, we fix, or try to fix, as much of standard number theory as possible.[55] We then twiddle the number 13 by assigning it the factors 2 and 6. One way to achieve this is to twiddle the multiplication function for 13. For instance, consider multiplication* that is just like the standard multiplication except that 2 multiply* 6 equals 13. We then examine the ramifications of this twiddle in the consequent of the countermathematical. Given that the consequent is about the life cycles of cicadas, this examination involves dealing with a physical or biological structure. This is where the issue of mathematical explanation becomes crucial.[56] For our purpose, however, we only need to understand how to twiddle 13 while holding the rest (as much as possible) of number theory fixed. It is here that impossible worlds become relevant since one might think that it is impossible for 13 not to be coprime with 2 and 3.

Impossibility involved in countermathematicals is just like the impossibility involved in counterlogicals. In a counterlogical, it is assumed that classical logic holds at the actual world. If the antecedent of a counterlogical involves a contradiction that is not accommodated by classical logic, it is considered to be impossible. Similarly, if the antecedent of a countermathematical involves a piece of mathematics that is not accommodated by the standard mathematics (or arithmetic in this case), it is considered to be impossible.

Thus, there are two ways to analyse the involvement of impossibility in evaluating a countermathematical. First, when we twiddle multiplication function, we might think of this twiddling to involve the change of the mathematical principle(s) governing multiplication for 13.[57] Given that we are holding the rest of number theory fixed, $2 \times 6 = 12$. But that contradicts the output of multiplication* for 2 and 6 as $2 \times^* 6 = 13$. In order to deal with this contradiction (and other contradictions), we might think of a world

---

[55] In a case of extra-mathematical explanation such as above, we also need to fix as much of physical or biological world as possible.

[56] For an intra-mathematical case which does not involve two kinds of structures but involve only mathematical structures, see Baron, Colyvan, & Ripley (2020).

[57] This is the twiddling Baron, Colyvan, & Ripley (2020) seem to recommend in the context of intra-mathematical cases.

where the antecedent of the countermathematical holds to be a world where a paraconsistent mathematics holds.[58] Given that a paraconsistent mathematics may behave just like classical mathematics in a consistent context,[59] we can simply allow those contradictions that arise explicitly from the particular twiddling of the mathematics in question but remain business as usual in doing (the rest of) mathematics.

Now, this way of twiddling involves worlds where a parconsistent mathematics holds. In evaluating our countermathematical, we can then consider a world where the antecedent holds to be a world that holds a different set of mathematical *principles* (or *rules*). In this case, we are holding fixed all of the mathematical *facts* except some facts about 13 but varying some of the principles. This means that we are invoking a mathematically different world to evaluate the countermathematical. If we think of a mathematically different world to be an impossible world just like a logically different world to be an impossible world, the kind of impossibility involved here ties impossibility to difference.

However, this is not the only way to understand twiddling of mathematics. So, second, we can fix mathematical principles but vary the facts about the factors of 13. We can do this by stipulating the fact about 2×6 to be 13 against the principles (or rules) for the standard multiplication function according to which $2 \times 6 = 12$.[60] In this case, we are allowing some mathematical facts to violate some of the mathematical principles. For instance, if we think of Peano Arithmetic, then the fact about the primeness of 13 under this assignment serves as a counterexample to the axioms of Peano Arithmetic that concern multiplication. So, in evaluating the countermathematical, we can think of invoking a world where mathematical principles or laws are violated in order to consider a situation where the antecedent holds.

It is when we consider impossibility in terms of violation that we can iron out the unnecessary contradictions that might arise in evaluating a countermathematical. To see this, consider the countermathematical: if $1 + 1 \neq 2$, then $2 + 1 \neq 3$.[61] In evaluating this, we have to suppose that there is a world where $1 + 1 \neq 2$. But if $1 + 1 \neq 2$, then, presumably, $1 + 1 + 2 \neq 4$. This contradicts our standard arithmetic according to which $1 + 1 + 2 = 4$. In order to manage the

---

[58] For paraconsistent mathematics, see Mortensen (1995), Priest (1997a, 2000, 2013), and Weber (2021).

[59] At least, that is what the behaviour of paraconsistent mathematics looks like from a classical perspective. See Weber (2021) for a discussion on this point.

[60] This is what Baron, Colyvan, & Ripley (2017) suggest we do in the case of the countermathematical in question.

[61] This example is discussed by Baron (2020: 541–542).

proliferation of contradictions that the impossibility of $1 + 1 \neq 2$ entails, we can stipulate that the standard arithmetical principles have a counterexample according to which the fact about $1 + 1 + 2$ is not 4. Since we are managing facts and not principles, no systematic adjustment is required. In this way, 'contradictions [can be] cleared from the neighbourhood of the [countermathematical] being evaluated' (Baron (2020: 542)). This clearing of contradictions is possible only if the impossibility of $1 + 1 \neq 2$ is understood as a violation of the standard arithmetic.[62]

7.4 Countermetafactuals, Countermetalogicals, and Countermetapossibles

Even after going through some forms of counterpossibles, counterlogicals and countermathematicals that are evaluated nonvacuously by making use of impossible worlds, one may not be persuaded to add impossible worlds in addition to possible worlds in order to evaluate the counterpossibles.[63] Moreover, one may insist that there is nothing wrong with evaluating all counterpossibles to be vacuously true. It might be thought that those who argue for nonvacuous evaluation of counterpossibles rely on their 'intuitions' to evaluate the truth values of various counterpossibles and use those intuitions to argue what the truth values of counterpossibles should be. But if one does not share the same intuitions, there may not be any reason to develop a method of nonvacuously evaluating counterpossibles (T. Williamson (2020, 2021)).[64]

However, regardless of what intuition one might have about various counterpossibles, there is good reason to think that not all counterpossibles should vacuously come out true. Consider the following conditionals:

(3) If Classical Logic were the correct logic, it would be impossible to validly infer every proposition from a contradiction.
(4) If LP were the correct logic, it would be impossible to validly infer every proposition from a contradiction.

These conditionals are crucial in logical disputes in which we debate about what the correct logic is or what logic holds at the actual world. If the dispute is genuine and the disputants are not talking past each other, it must be understood

---

[62] While we have no desire to jump into the fray, we note that this analysis of countermathematicals as involving violations of standard mathematics answers some of the objections raised by Kasirzadeh (2023) which rely on the idea that mathematics is systematic and, thus, contradictions cannot be ironed out.

[63] This is so especially because there is a way of accounting for counterpossibles without introducing impossible worlds (French, Girard, & Ripley (2022)).

[64] We will get back to this in §8.

what it would be for those conditionals to hold. This is the case even if one is convinced that classical logic or LP is not the correct logic.[65]

From a classical perspective, it may *not* be impossible for LP to hold at the actual world. As we have seen before, LP is a sublogic of classical logic. So the theorems of LP form a subset of the theorems of classical logic. From a classical perspective, then, LP may be non-true since it is deficient in accounting all of the valid inferences but it is not necessarily an impossibility. However, from a perspective of LP, it is impossible for ECQ to be valid as LP invalidates it. So, from LP's perspective, it is impossible for classical logic to hold at the actual world. From LP's perspective, then, the antecedent of (3) is an impossibility. However, every proposition can be classically inferred from a contradiction. So, (3) should be non-true even if the antecedent may be impossible. Even though this reasoning is conducted from LP's perspective, it is a perfectly legitimate reasoning from a classical perspective as LP is a sublogic of classical logic and so the reasoning does not involve any invalid moves from a classical perspective. Hence, even classically, not all counterpossibles should be declared to be vacuously true.

Now, the above conditionals are examples of what we call *countermetalogicals* (Sandgren & Tanaka (2020)).[66] Countermetalogicals are a special kind of counterlogicals. The difference between counterlogicals and countermetalogicals turns on how logical impossibility is involved. A countermetalogical like (3) and (4) is true in case the following holds: *if* the logic mentioned in the antecedent holds at the actual world, then there would be no worlds, most-similar to the actual world, in which we could validly infer a certain inference mentioned in the consequent. So an evaluation of a countermetalogical requires two steps. For instance, in evaluating (3), first, we suppose that the actual laws of logic (the laws of logic that hold at the actual world) are classical. This requires a suspension of our prejudgement about what logic holds at the actual world as we are only supposing what logic holds at the actual world. Based on this supposition, we order all the worlds in terms of 'similarity'. Then, second, we evaluate whether or not it is impossible to validly infer every proposition from a contradiction at the worlds most-similar to the actual world. Given that a countermetalogical is concerned with the correct laws of logic (the logical laws that hold at the actual world), the worlds most similar to the actual world are classical worlds in considering (3). Since ECQ is classically valid, it cannot be

---

[65] See also Berto & Jago (2019: 176) and Priest (2016a: §3.3).

[66] This terminology was originally borrowed from Kocurek & Jerzak (2021). It should be noted, though, that what they mean by countermetalogicals is close to what we mean by counterlogicals as we will see below.

impossible to validly infer every proposition from a contradiction at classical worlds. Hence, (3) is non-true.

Analysed in this way, we can see that an evaluation of a countermetalogical invokes two kinds of impossibility. (i) In identifying the most-similar worlds to be classical worlds, we presuppose that there are various logically different worlds. So if it is impossible to validly infer every proposition from a contradiction, then that would be a world logically different from the actual world. (ii) But if it is impossible to validly infer every proposition from a contradiction at the most-similar classical worlds to the actual world, that must be because those worlds go against the actual laws of logic. So the impossibility embedded in the consequent appeals to logical violations. Thus, to make sense of countermetalogicals, we need to make room for two kinds of impossibility.

In contrast, an evaluation of a counterlogical does not require these two steps. In a counterlogical such as

> If I had found Sylvan's Box which is and is not empty, I would have made a space ship and sent it into orbit.

the antecedent concerns a matter of fact. If an impossibility is involved, it is the fact expressed in the antecedent that violates the actual law. So a counterlogical invokes only the sense of impossibility tied to violation.[67]

7.5 Causal Counterfactuals

The last type of the family of counterfactuals/counterpossibles we consider is somewhat metaphysical. It concerns causal matters, in particular the connection between causation and counterfactuals under the assumption that determinism holds.[68] There is what Nolan (2017) calls the *deviation problem* in considering counterfactuals whose antecedent represents or expresses a state that deviates from the actual state and whose consequent represents or expresses a state that obtains later than the antecedent state. It is a problem associated with answering the question: what differences do we need to accommodate in evaluating such causal counterfactuals? For instance, consider the following counterfactual:

> If I had skipped breakfast, I would have had more to eat at lunch.
> (Nolan (2017: 16))

If we are to evaluate it in terms of the closest worlds where the antecedent is true just like the standard semantics for counterfactuals in the style of

---

[67] What Kocurek & Jerzak (2021) call countermetalogicals involve only logical violations. So, their countermetalogicals are our counterlogicals.

[68] A similar issue arises in the context of indeterminism; however, for an illustrative purpose, we confine ourselves to determinism.

Kratzer/Lewis/Stalnaker, what are the closest worlds be like where I skipped breakfast? Beside skipping breakfast, what other deviations should there be?

There are generally two ways to understand the required deviations. First, we can understand them in terms of different facts (though as close to the actual facts as possible) while maintaining the same laws. Second, we can understand the required deviations in terms of different laws of nature (at least those that pertain to causation) while fixing the (contingent) facts as close to those of the actual world as possible. The first approach involves what Nolan (2017) calls impossible worlds. The second approach gives rise to *miracles* (Lewis (1979, 1981)). (No wonder no one seems happy with any proposal.) In this section, we will provide an analysis of these two approaches by appealing to different ways of understanding impossible worlds as we saw in Sections 3–6 (though we do not even attempt to settle the issue about the connection between counterfactuals and causation). We will see that both approaches are essentially impossible worlds approaches but they appeal to different kinds of impossible worlds.

Nolan (2017) introduces the impossible world approach to account for the closest worlds where the antecedent holds differently from the miracle approach. He specifies four conditions on the closest worlds that are relevant to evaluating the causal counterfactuals such as above. Let w be a world where a causal counterfactual is true and w^* a closest world where the antecedent is true. Then, (1) the laws of nature (or the laws of physics) that hold at w also hold at w^*, (2) all of the truths that hold before time t at w are also the truths that hold before t at w^*, (3) there is no proposition at w^* that expresses that the laws of nature are violated (Nolan (2017: 26)). It is also assumed (4) that the facts that hold after t at w^* are constrained or governed by the laws of nature under consideration. (2) ensures that all of the truths up to t hold at w^* if they hold at w. So we have worlds that have the same history up to t. (3) implies that w^* does not 'say of itself' that it has counterexamples. This is the case even if there are, in fact, counterexamples.[69]

Now, (1) together with (4) implies that the laws of nature (or the laws of physics) at w^* are the same as those that hold at w. This means that w and w^* are *not* physically different worlds as the same laws hold at both of those worlds. Nevertheless, w^* may be an impossible world as it may contain a counterexample to the laws. For Nolan, this means that w^* is not closed under logical

---

[69] Nolan (2017) thinks of what we call the counterexamples in terms of inconsistency: 'a certain past ... is strictly inconsistent with a certain body of laws of nature' (p. 26). Given that we are concerned with logic-neutral definition of impossible worlds, we generalise such inconsistency to a 'mismatch' between 'a certain past' and the laws of nature, that is, a counterexample.

consequence. In other words, it is an open world. He does not say what exactly he means by an open world. But, an open world in this sense must be a silent world (where the world is silent about the consequence relation between some facts) or an anarchic world (where the facts may behave against the laws) as some laws of nature do hold at the world.

Crucially, since w^* has the same laws of nature as w, no physically different worlds (worlds that have different laws of nature) are involved. And, because it is an open world, the mismatch between some (past) facts and the laws may not trivialise the world even when these worlds are understood from a perspective of classical logic. The advantage of this approach is that it does not involve miracles to which we now turn.

To examine the miracle approach, consider two worlds w_0 and w_1 that are exactly the same until shortly before time t. That is, w_0 and w_1 have exactly the same facts until shortly before t. However, shortly before t, an event takes place that violates the laws of nature. This event is said to be a miracle or a 'tiny miracle' (D. Lewis (1979: 468)) because 'whatever else a law may be, it is at least an exceptionless regularity' (D. Lewis (1979: 468–469)). After the miracle, w_0 and w_1 diverge and some event may take place in w_1 after t that does not take place in w_0.

Now, Lewis explains that a miracle that takes place in w_1 is a violation of the laws of nature that hold at w_0. This means that a miracle in w_1 violates the laws of nature in w_0 and, thus, it is a miracle relative to w_0. Crucially, he claims that the laws at w_0 are 'at best the almost-laws of w_1' and that '[t]he laws of w_1 itself, if such there be, do not enter into it' (D. Lewis (1979: 469)). This suggests that it is not only that different facts obtain at w_1 after t but that different laws hold at t (and, perhaps, after t). So, w_0 and w_1 are different with respect to the laws.[70] Thus, the miracle approach is an impossible world approach given our discussion of impossible worlds in Sections 3–6. However, it invokes a different kind of impossible worlds from the impossible world approach of Nolan discussed above. A miracle world is different (from another world such as the actual world) not only with respect to factual matters but also with respect to the laws. It makes use of the notion of difference in addition to the notion of violation.

8 Representation

Applications of impossible worlds often concern *representation*. Typically, it is these applications that are used to motivate adding impossible worlds

---

[70] For this analysis, see Nolan (2017) and T. L. Williamson & Sandgren (2021).

to the worlds framework. We have already encountered some of them. In examining open worlds in §4, we considered intentional states such as beliefs and knowledge. We saw that those mental states might not be closed under logical consequence and we examined how best to understand open worlds and whether openness should be considered as characterisitc of impossible worlds. Representing such intentional states seems to require impossible worlds in addition to possible worlds.

Counterpossibles and their variants that we saw in §7 also concern representation. In evaluating a counterpossible nonvacuously using a worlds-based framework, we consider the worlds where the antecedent is true. In so doing, we are taking the worlds to be representing the impossible antecedent. So, if we think that counterpossibles need to be nonvacuously evaluated, impossibillity must be thought to be represented since the antecedent of a counterpossible is meant to be impossible. Given that counterpossibles and their variants are important applications of impossible worlds (§7), representation has been crucial for motivating and legitimising the use of impossible worlds.

The applications of impossible worlds that concern representation include analyses of information, content (such as propositional content), imagination, fiction, as well as belief, knowledge, and counterpossibles. Impossible worlds allow for finer-grained distinctions than are possible if we are limited to the space of possible worlds.[71] For instance, we seem to be able to believe that p without believing that q even if p and q are true at all the same possible worlds (i.e., equivalent) as the example in Introduction illustrates:

(i) If you apply for the job, you have a 80 per cent chance of not getting it.
(ii) If you apply for the job, you have a 20 per cent chance of getting it.

Impossible worlds allow the contents of these beliefs to come apart and, thus, allow for distinctions between many representational contents that are conflated on coarser-grained conceptions of the contents of representations.

In this Element, we are not going to examine all of these applications in the context of representation. This is partly because of the lack of space but mainly because we have, albeit briefly in some cases, dealt with some of the main applications already such as belief, knowledge and counterpossibles. Instead, in this final section, we will consider some challenges to the view that allow for fine-grained representation. We will not silence the challenges; however, we will point out what is at stake in the debate.

In introducing impossible worlds, it is common to assume unrestricted comprehension: for any A, there is at least one world where A holds and there is

---

at least one world where A fails (Nolan (1997), Priest (2016a)).[72] Unrestricted comprehension places very few, if any, constraints on the worlds. As we saw in §3.3, an implication is that LHS fails as unrestricted comprehension allows two worlds to be the same with respect to the laws but differ with respect to their instances. This means that the 'space' of worlds that includes impossible worlds (to be metaphorical) is massively unconstrained.

If we use worlds to capture the content of representations, the resulting conception of content is extremely fine-grained. It allows for distinctions between many contents that are conflated on coarser-grained conceptions of the contents of representations. If we allow, as we have suggested, that worlds differ with respect to which laws hold at the world, even if the rest of the worlds are the same, we allow for even more fine-grained content than is typically acknowledged in the literature. Given unrestricted comprehension, representation becomes as fine-grained as the language we use for it as there is a world for each A (Berto & Jago (2019: §8.4)).[73]

This unconstrained modal space that allows for fine-grained representation may be challenged in two ways. First, it might be thought that if representational content (what is believed, what is known, what is said, etc.) becomes too fine-grained, it threatens plausible accounts of interpersonal phenomena such as communication, agreement (and disagreement), meaning, essentially all of the things that seem to require representing the same content. We often say the same thing, believe the same thing, know the same thing, so we think. A natural way to account for this is to appeal to shared contents. The reason why you and I believe the same thing is that there is a content that we *both* believe. If we allow for too many distinctions between contents, it is difficult to account for the shared content since any minute difference may split the shared content apart.[74]

More specifically, a popular model of communication has it that successful communication involves a speaker expressing a belief and the audience coming to have a belief with the same content. If the contents of mental representations like beliefs are allowed to be too fine-grained, this kind of correspondence will be uncommon. So, if we allow for too fine-grained distinctions, communication will also be uncommon. But communication is not uncommon. So, one might think, either this model of communication is inaccurate or representational content is relatively coarse-grained. Some take this to be a good reason to

---

[72] This is a strong form of unrestricted comprehension. See §3.3.

[73] There is a way of using impossible worlds to give contents of sentences that stops short of being as fine-grained as the syntax. See Fouché (2022). Thanks go to an anonymous reviewer for the reference.

[74] See Bjerring & Schwarz (2017).

reject fine-grained conceptions of representation (Bjerring & Schwarz (2017), Elliot (2019), Stalnaker (1981, 2008)). Similar considerations apply to agreement (and disagreement), meaning and all other issues of representation that seem to require representing the same content.

Second, the introduction of impossible worlds may not only make it hard to account for interpersonal phenomena but they may make representation unsystematic. We saw in §5 that if we identify an impossible world as a world that contains violation, there are counterexamples to the laws. If there are counterexamples, there are some instances of the laws that go against the laws. And, if there are such instances, a specification or description of a world cannot simply be read off the laws. This means that what a world represents may not be downstream from the laws. So, if we introduce impossible worlds, in addition to possible worlds, to account for representation, what a world represents may not always be systematic.[75] This means that, to a certain extent, the details of worlds will have to be filled in 'by hand' rather than derived in a systematic way from the laws. If there are instances of the laws that violate the laws, what happens at a world may not cooperate with the laws. Then, some facts that obtain at the world may need to be written by hand (so to speak) as they are not entailed by the laws. Hence, an account of representation that systematically accounts for representation by appealing to logical laws or rules may not be forthcoming.[76]

In response to these challenges, one can either (1) give up on impossible worlds and the fine-grain distinctions that they afford or (2) bite the bullet and suggest alternative accounts of representation that may sacrifice simple and systematic accounts of various representational phenomena. Opting for (2) faces the challenge from *overfitting* (T. Williamson (2020: ch. 15, 2021)). A theory overfits the data if it can fit any data including outlying data. Williamson argues that accommodating the fine-grained distinctions that impossible worlds allow is a case of overfitting. Consider, for example, the following two sentences:

(1) Richard brought it about that Edward was a king.
(2) Richard brought it about that Edward was a male monarch.

where Richard is Richard Neville, Duke of Warwick, and Edward is Edward Plantagent, who became King Edward IV (T. Williamson (2021: 89)). Since (1) and (2) are historical facts, we might be inclined to assess (1) and (2) as both true. Moreover, 'king' is synonymous with 'male monarch'. So (1) and (2) must

---

[75] One can achieve the same effect without adding impossible worlds. See Berto (2021, 2022).

[76] For a similar concern, see Berto & Jago (2019: §8.4).

be equivalent. However, Edward being a male was not Richard's making. So (2) cannot be true because 'brought it about' must be understood causally. We might then be tempted to think that this is a case where fine-grained distinctions (hyperintentionality) must be accommodated. But, as Williamson responds, this is a case where 'superficial linguistic features' (T. Williamson (2021: 89)) of the sentences misleads us to think that (2) is true. If we read (2) as a causal claim, there is no mystery to be solved, so Williamson argues.

It is not clear whether or not all the examples that have been thought to give rise to fine-grained distinctions or hyperintentionality can be analysed away in the way that Williamson recommends. However, the use of impossible worlds may require some major changes to the way in which we can capture representational contents. While we do not offer our own account of representation here,[77] our discussion of representation reveals what is at stake in continuing to embrace impossible worlds. In this Element, we have shown what impossible worlds are and can do as well as the advantages of adopting impossible worlds. However, this is not the end of the road and there is a lot more to be discussed. It is hoped that this Element opens up more avenues for debate.

---

[77] For some of the alternative accounts of various representational phenomena, see, for instance, Badura & Berto (2018), Berto & Jago (2019: chs. 9, 10, 11), Girard & Tanaka (2016), Jago (2013a, 2014), and Priest (2005).

References

Badura, C., & Berto, F. (2018). 'Truth in Fiction, Impossible Worlds, and Belief Revision'. *Australasian Journal of Philosophy*, *97*(1), 178–193.

Baker, A. (2005). 'Are There Genuine Mathematical Explanations of Physical Phenomena?'. *Mind*, *114*(454), 223–238.

Baker, A. (2009). 'Mathematical Explanation in Science'. *British Journal for the Philosophy of Science*, *60*(3), 611–633.

Baker, A. (2017a). 'Mathematical Spandrels'. *Australasian Journal of Philosophy*, *95*(4), 779–793.

Baker, A. (2017b). 'Mathematics and Explanatory Generality'. *Philosophia Mathematica*, *25*(2), 194–209.

Baker, A., & Colyvan, M. (2011). 'Indexing and Mathematical Explanation'. *Philosophia Mathematica*, *19*, 323–334.

Baron, S. (2020). 'Counterfactual Scheming'. *Mind*, *129*(514), 535–562.

Baron, S., Colyvan, M., & Ripley, D. (2017). 'How Mathematics Can Make a Difference?'. *Philosophers' Imprint*, *17*(3).

Baron, S., Colyvan, M., & Ripley, D. (2020). 'A Counterfactual Approach to Explanation in Mathematics'. *Philosophia Mathematica*, *28*(1), 1–34.

Barwise, J. (1989). *The Situation in Logic*. Stanford: CSLI.

Barwise, J., & Perry, J. (1983). *Situations and Attitudes*. Cambridge, MA: MIT Press.

Beall, J., & Restall, G. (2006). *Logical Pluralism*. Oxford: Oxford University Press.

Bernstein, S. (2016). 'Omission Impossible'. *Philosophical Studies*, *173*, 2575–2589.

Berto, F. (2021). 'Equivalence in Imagination'. In C. Badura, & E. Kind (Eds.), *Epistemic Uses of Imagination* (pp. 122–140). New York: Routledge.

Berto, F. (2022). *Topics of Thought*. Oxford: Oxford University Press.

Berto, F., French, R., Priest, G., & Ripley, D. (2018). 'Williamson on Counterpossibles'. *Journal of Philosophical Logic*, *47*, 693–713.

Berto, F., & Jago, M. (2019). *Impossible Worlds*. Oxford: Oxford University Press.

Berto, F., & Jago, M. (2022). 'Impossible Worlds'. In E. N. Zalta, & U. Nodelman (Eds.), *The Stanford Encyclopedia of Philosophy* (Winter 2022 ed.). Metaphysics Research Lab, Stanford University. https://plato.stanford.edu/archives/win2022/entries/impossible-worlds/.

Berto, F., & Nolan, D. (2021). 'Hyperintensionality'. In E. N. Zalta (Ed.), *The Stanford Encyclopedia of Philosophy* (Summer 2021 ed.). Metaphysics Research Lab, Stanford University. https://plato.stanford.edu/archives/sum2021/entries/hyperintensionality/.

Bjerring, J. C. (2013). 'Impossible Worlds and Logical Omniscience: An Impossibility Result'. *Synthese*, *190*, 2505–2524.

Bjerring, J. C. (2014). 'On Counterpossibles'. *Philosophical Studies*, *168*, 327–353.

Bjerring, J. C., & Schwarz, W. (2017). 'Granularity Problems'. *Philosophical Quarterly*, *67*(266), 22–37.

Cotnoir, A. (2018). 'Logical Nihilism'. In N. Kellen, N. Pedersen, & J. Wyatt (Eds.), *Pluralisms in Truth and Logic* (pp. 301–329). London: Palgrave Macmillan.

Cresswell, M. (1995). 'S1 Is Not So Simple'. In E. Sinnott-Armstrong, D. Raffiman, & N. Asher (Eds.), *Modality, Morality and Belief: Essays in Honor of Ruth Barcan Marcus* (pp. 29–40). Cambridge: Cambridge University Press.

Elliot, E. (2019). 'Impossible Worlds and Partial Beliefs'. *Synthese*, *196*, 3433–3458.

Estrada-González, L. (2012). 'Models of Possibilism and Trivialism'. *Logic and Logical Philosophy*, *21*(2), 175–205.

Fouché, C. (2022). 'Hybrid Modal Realism Debugged'. *Erkenntnis*, Online First.

French, R., Girard, P., & Ripley, D. (2022). 'Classical Counterpossibles'. *The Review of Symbolic Logic*, *15*(1), 259–275.

Girard, P., & Tanaka, K. (2016). 'Paraconsistent Dynamics'. *Synthese*, *193*(1), 1–14.

Goodman, J. (2004). 'An Extended Lewis/Stalnaker Semantics and the New Problem of Counterpossibles'. *Philosophical Papers*, *33*(1), 35–66.

Hintikka, J. (1962). *Knowledge and Belief*. Ithaca: Carnell University Press.

Jacob, P. (2023). 'Intentionality'. In E. N. Zalta, & U. Nodelman (Eds.), *The Stanford Encyclopedia of Philosophy* (Spring 2023 ed.). Metaphysics Research Lab, Stanford University. https://plato.stanford.edu/archives/spr2023/entries/intentionality/.

Jago, M. (2007). 'Hintikka and Cresswell on Logical Omniscience'. *Logic and Logical Philosophy*, *15*, 325–354.

Jago, M. (2009). 'Logical Information and Epistemic Space'. *Synthese*, *167*, 327–341.

Jago, M. (2013a). 'The Content of Deduction'. *Journal of Philosophical Logic*, *42*, 317–334.

Jago, M. (2013b). 'Impossible Worlds'. *Noûs*, *47*, 713–728.

Jago, M. (2014). *The Impossible*. Oxford: Oxford University Press.

Kabay, P. (2010). *On the Plenitude of Truth: A Defense of Trivialism*. London: Lambert Academic.

Kasirzadeh, A. (2023). 'Counter Countermathematical Explanations'. *Erkenntnis*, *88*, 2537–2560.

Kiourti, I. (2019). 'An Excess of Dialetheias: In Defence of Genuine Impossible Worlds'. In A. Rieger, & G. Young (Eds.), *Dialetheism and Its Applications* (pp. 81–100). Cham: Springer.

Kocurek, A., & Jerzak, E. (2021). 'Counterlogicals as Counterconventionals'. *Journal of Philosophical Logic*, *50*, 673–704.

Kouri Kissel, T. (2019). 'Metalinguistic Negotiation and Logical Pluralism'. *Synthese*, *198*(Suppl 20), 4801–4812.

Kratzer, A. (1977). 'What "Must" and "Can" Must and Can Mean'. *Linguistics and Philosophy*, *1*(3), 337–355.

Kripke, S. (1965). 'Semantical Analysis of Modal Logic II. Non-Normal Modal Propositional Calculi'. In J. Addison, L. Henkin, & A. Tarski (Eds.), *The Theory of Models* (pp. 206–220). Amsterdam: North-Holland.

Lemmon, E. J. (1957). 'New Foundations for Lewis Modal Systems'. *The Journal of Symbolic Logic*, *22*, 176–186.

Lewis, C. I. (1918). *A Survey of Symbolic Logic*. Berkeley: University of California Press.

Lewis, D. (1973). *Counterfactuals*. Oxford: Blackwell.

Lewis, D. (1979). 'Counterfactual Dependence and Time's Arrow'. *Noûs*, *13*, 455–476.

Lewis, D. (1981). 'Are We Free to Break the Laws?'. *Theoria*, *47*, 113–121.

Lewis, D. (1986). *Philosophical Papers* (Vol. 2). Oxford: Oxford University Press.

Lynch, M. (2009). *Truth as One and Many*. Oxford: Oxford University Press.

Mares, E. (1997). 'Who's Afraids of Impossible Worlds?'. *Notre Dame Journal of Formal Logic*, *38*, 516–526.

Mortensen, C. (1989). 'Anything Is Possible'. *Erkenntnis*, *30*, 319–337.

Mortensen, C. (1995). *Inconsistent Mathematics*. Dordrecht: Kluwer.

Nolan, D. (1997). 'Impossible Worlds: A Modest Approach'. *Notre Dame Journal of Formal Logic*, *38*, 535–572.

Nolan, D. (2013). 'Impossible Worlds'. *Philosophy Compass*, *8*, 360–372.

Nolan, D. (2014). 'Hyperintensional Metaphysics'. *Philosophical Studies*, *171*(1), 149–160.

Nolan, D. (2017). 'Causal Counterfactuals and Impossible Worlds'. In H. Beebee, C. Hitchcock, & H. Price (Eds.), *Making a Difference: Essays on the Philosophy of Causation* (pp. 14–32). Oxford: Oxford University Press.

Priest, G. (1979). 'Logic of Paradox'. *Journal of Philosophical Logic, 8*, 219–241.

Priest, G. (1992). 'What Is a Non-Normal World?'. *Logique et Analyse, 35*, 291–302.

Priest, G. (1997a). 'Inconsistent Models of Arithmetic Part I: Finite Models'. *Journal of Philosophical Logic, 26*(2), 223–235.

Priest, G. (1997b). 'Sylvan's Box'. *Notre Dame Journal of Formal Logic, 38*(4), 573–582.

Priest, G. (2000). 'Inconsistent Models of Arithmetic Part II: The General Case'. *The Journal of Symbolic Logic, 65*(4), 1519–1529.

Priest, G. (2001). 'Logic: One or Many?'. In J. Woods, & B. Brown (Eds.), *Logical Consequences: Rival Approaches* (pp. 23–38). Oxford: Hermes Scientific.

Priest, G. (2005). *Towards Non-Being*. Oxford: Oxford University Press.

Priest, G. (2008). *An Introduction to Non-Classical Logic* (2nd ed.). Cambridge: Cambridge University Press.

Priest, G. (2013). 'Mathematical Pluralism'. *Logic Journal of the IGPL, 21*(1), 4–13.

Priest, G. (2016a). 'Thinking the Impossible'. *Philosophical Studies, 173*, 2649–2662.

Priest, G. (2016b). *Towards Non-Being* (2nd ed.). Oxford: Oxford University Press.

Priest, G. (202+). 'Mission Impossible'. In Y. Weiss, & R. Padró (Eds.), *Saul Kripke on Modal Logic*. New York: Springer.

Priest, G., Tanaka, K., & Weber, Z. (2022). 'Paraconsistent Logic'. In E. N. Zalta, & U. Nodelman (Eds.), *The Stanford Encyclopedia of Philosophy* (Spring 2022 ed.). Metaphysics Research Lab, Stanford University. https://plato.stanford.edu/entries/logic-paraconsistent/.

Rantala, V. (1982a). 'Impossible Worlds Semantics and Logical Omniscience'. *Acta Philosophica Fennica, 35*, 18–24.

Rantala, V. (1982b). 'Quantified Modal Logic: Non-Normal Worlds and Propositional Attitudes'. *Studia Logica, 41*, 41–65.

Restall, G. (1997). 'Ways Things Can't Be'. *Notre Dame Journal of Formal Logic, 38*(4), 583–596.

Routley, R., & Meyer, R. (1973). 'The Semantics of Entailment – I'. In H. Leblanc (Ed.), *Truth, Syntax and Modality* (pp. 199–243). Amsterdam: North-Holland.

Routley, R., Plumwood, V., Meyer, R. K., & Brady, R. T. (1982). *Relevant Logics and Their Rivals*. Atascadero: Ridgeview.

Routley, R., & Routley, V. (1972). 'The Semantics of First Degree Entailment'. *Noûs*, 6, 335–359.

Russell, G. (2008). 'One True Logic?'. *Journal of Philosophical Logic*, 37(6), 593–611.

Russell, G. (2017). 'An Introduction to Logical Nihilism'. In H. Leitgeb, I. Niiniluoto, P. Seppälä, & E. Sober (Eds.), *Logic, Methodology and Philosophy of Science – Proceedings of the 15th International Congress* (pp. 125–135). London: College Publications.

Russell, G. (2018). 'Logical Nihilism: Could There Be No Logic?'. *Philosophical Issues*, 28, 308–324.

Sandgren, A., & Tanaka, K. (2020). 'Two Kinds of Logical Impossibility'. *Noûs*, 54(4), 795–806.

Stalnaker, R. (1968). 'A Theory of Conditionals'. In N. Rescher (Ed.), *Studies in Logical Theory* (pp. 98–112). Oxford: Blackwell.

Stalnaker, R. (1981). 'Indexical Belief'. *Synthese*, 49, 129–151.

Stalnaker, R. (2008). *Our Knowledge of the Internal World*. Oxford: Oxford University Press.

Tanaka, K. (2013). 'Making Sense of Paraconsistent Logic: The Nature of Logic, Classical Logic and Paraconsistent Logic'. In K. Tanaka, F. Berto, E. Mares, and F. Paoli *et al.* (Eds.), *Paraconsistency: Logic and Applications* (pp. 15–25). Dordrecht: Springer.

Tanaka, K. (2018). 'Logically Impossible Worlds'. *Australasian Journal of Logic*, 15(2), 489–497.

Tanaka, K. (202+). *'Impossibility Happens!'*. (A paper presented to the 2023 Australasian Association of Philosophy conference.)

Tanaka, K., & Girard, P. (2023). 'Against Classical Paraconsistent Metatheory'. *Analysis*, 83(2), 285–294.

Tversky, A., & Kahneman, D. (1981). 'The Framing of Decisions and the Psychology of Choice'. *Science*, 211, 453–458.

Vander Laan, D. (1997). 'The Ontology of Impossible Worlds'. *Notre Dame Journal of Formal Logic*, 38, 597–620.

Weber, Z. (2021). *Paradoxes and Inconsistent Mathematics*. Cambridge: Cambridge University Press.

Weber, Z., & Omori, H. (2019). 'Observations on the Trivial World'. *Erkenntnis*, 84, 975–994.

Williamson, T. (2007). *The Philosophy of Philosophy*. Oxford: Oxford University Press.

Williamson, T. (2010). 'Modal Logic Within Counterfactual Logic'. In B. Hale and A. Hoffmann (Eds.), *Modality: Metaphysics, Logic, and Epistemology* (pp. 81–96). Oxford: Oxford University Press.

Williamson, T. (2013). *Modal Logic as Metaphysics*. Oxford: Oxford University Press.

Williamson, T. (2020). *Suppose and Tell*. Oxford: Oxford University Press.

Williamson, T. (2021). 'Degrees of Freedom: Is Good Philosophy Bad Science?'. *Disputatio, 13*(61), 73–94.

Williamson, T. L., & Sandgren, A. (2021). 'Law-Abiding Causal Decision Theory'. *The British Journal for the Philosophy of Science*, Online First.

Yagisawa, T. (2010). *Worlds and Individuals*. Oxford: Oxford University Press.

Zalta, E. (1997). 'A Classically-Based Theory of Impossible Worlds'. *Notre Dame Journal of Formal Logic, 38*, 640–660.

Acknowledgements

We would like to thank the graduate students in our Foundations Seminars in the School of Philosophy at the Australian National University for discussing the materials used in the Element with us. Lively conversations we had in and out of classroom were not only enjoyable but valuable. Many thanks also go to Francesco Berto, Daniel Nolan, and Graham Priest with whom we discussed many issues about impossible worlds as well as Mark Colyvan and Alan Háyek for their comments on some parts of an earlier draft of the Element. We would also like to thank two anonymous reviewers for Cambridge University Press for their comments which led to many improvements and the series editors Bradley Armour-Garb and Fred Kroon for inviting us to write this Element. Koji Tanaka is supported by an Australian Research Council Future Fellowship (FT160100360).

Cambridge Elements ≡

Philosophy and Logic

Bradley Armour-Garb

SUNY Albany

Brad Armour-Garb is chair and Professor of Philosophy at SUNY Albany. His books include *The Law of Non-Contradiction* (co-edited with Graham Priest and J. C. Beall, 2004), *Deflationary Truth* and *Deflationism and Paradox* (both co-edited with J. C. Beall, 2005), *Pretense and Pathology* (with James Woodbridge, Cambridge University Press, 2015), *Reflections on the Liar* (2017), and *Fictionalism in Philosophy* (co-edited with Fred Kroon, 2020).

Frederick Kroon

The University of Auckland

Frederick Kroon is Emeritus Professor of Philosophy at the University of Auckland. He has authored numerous papers in formal and philosophical logic, ethics, philosophy of language, and metaphysics, and is the author of *A Critical Introduction to Fictionalism* (with Stuart Brock and Jonathan McKeown-Green, 2018).

About the Series

This Cambridge Elements series provides an extensive overview of the many and varied connections between philosophy and logic. Distinguished authors provide an up-to-date summary of the results of current research in their fields and give their own take on what they believe are the most significant debates influencing research, drawing original conclusions.

Printed in the United States
by Baker & Taylor Publisher Services